CREATING YOUR DOJO

Keep fostering
learning.

[signature]

Amy —
KEEP WORKING
ON HELPING PEOPLE LEARN!

REN

[signature]

CREATING YOUR

DOJO

Upskill Your Organization for Digital Evolution

DION STEWART & JOEL TOSI

LIONCREST

PUBLISHING

CREATING YOUR DOJO

Upskill Your Organization for Digital Evolution

ISBN   978-1-5445-0439-1 *Paperback*

978-1-5445-0440-7 *Ebook*

From Dion:

For Marie, who never questioned my ability to pull this off. Thank you for your friendship and love.

From Joel:

For my amazing wife, Rinda, who listens to my crazy ideas and never hesitates to support them all. And, to my kids, Mira, Ian, and Kara, for keeping me young and being the best distractions to writing imaginable. I love you all.

CONTENTS

INTRODUCTION

Long-term commitment to new learning and new philosophy is required of any management that seeks transformation. The timid and the fainthearted, and people that expect quick results, are doomed to disappointment.

—W. EDWARDS DEMING, *OUT OF THE CRISIS*

"The coupons still aren't working. The test cases are failing. Your code is wrong!"

"Your testing script is wrong. The code is written to spec. If you have a problem, go talk to the business!"

Joan, the payments team leader, rose from her desk and went to see what the commotion was about. One of her team's developers was facing off with one of the test engineers in the hallway. The test engineer rolled his eyes and shook his head at the developer. When Joan asked them what the problem was, the tester said the new coupons still weren't working correctly, but that the developer kept rejecting defects in the defect tracking system. They were at an impasse.

Joan was questioning her decision to accept the promotion to team leader she'd taken a couple months ago. She had been up late the previous night with her developers and people from operations trying to get their code deployed in the staging environment. Now it appeared the code was wrong and she might have another late night ahead of her doing another deployment. That assumed they could get one of their business partners to clarify how the coupons should work and get the code changes made today. As if that wasn't enough, she had a meeting in the afternoon with the stakeholders to explain why they were so far behind schedule. At a minimum, they were looking at another day of delay.

She was extremely frustrated. The codebase her team had inherited made it difficult to add new functionality with any kind of code quality. They rarely met delivery deadlines. Even though her company had sent hundreds of people through Agile training that advocated for cross-functional teams, her part of the organization was still siloed, with separate development teams and test teams. She couldn't put together a team with the skills she knew would address at least a few of their problems.

Even worse, new features weren't having the impact in the marketplace the business wanted. Her developers wanted time to clean up technical debt in the codebase, but the business just wanted more features faster, hoping they'd somehow achieve product/market fit. On top of all that, the organization mandated that all the services her team owned had to be moved to the cloud by the end of the year.

Something had to change.

Joan believed in her team's abilities, but she wasn't sure how they could make improvements with all the pressure they were under to constantly deliver. A few of her developers had attended a test-driven development course but that didn't seem to go anywhere because they'd had a hard time applying what they learned to their legacy codebase. There were several other two-day training courses her team members could attend, but she was skeptical there would be any real long-term impact.

She'd heard rumblings that her company had recently hired a new director of IT transformation and that he was creating something called a dojo to help teams get better at building digital products. She decided she'd look into it.

Does Joan's story sound familiar? Read on.

WHAT'S A DOJO, YOU ASK?

A dojo is an immersive learning environment within an organization where product teams learn new skills and new ways to solve problems. Teams apply those skills immediately to their work in the context of their real-world constraints and challenges. "Dojo" is a Japanese term for meditation halls and martial arts studios. It translates literally as "place of the way." In the tech industry, dojos are pointing the way to better products and methods, and more effective problem-solving and learning within organizations. Dojos are leading organizational and cultural transformations.

Unlike traditional training where individuals or teams go to a conference or seminar, or external consultants come into the organization to conduct workshops, a dojo is a space unto itself within an organization, run by dedicated employees of the organization. It goes beyond the in-house training centers that teach one-off skills.

A dojo is an investment for the organization—in people, space, and time. For small organizations (with, say, less than four or five product teams)—a physical dojo space may be overkill, but the approach to learning presented in this book still applies.

For large organizations, an investment in a dojo starts with an honest conversation around whether a dojo can meet the needs of the organization. This ultimately comes down to whether there is executive-level support for evolution through learning. If your leadership believes in investing in your people and giving them time to improve their skills, then you are ready to start looking into a dojo. On the other hand, if leadership believes in a guaranteed transformation through large consulting firms with fancy frameworks telling you what to do—well, history tells you how that story ends.

When an organization invests in a dojo, it becomes an attractor for new talent. Perceptions about the company shift within the development community. People recognize the company is doing something new and interesting. More importantly, it becomes clear that the company is investing in developing their people.

If you decide to add a dojo to your organization, you probably have people who can fill the various roles in your organization already. You might have to hire outside consultants in the beginning to get your dojo up and running. But let's not get ahead of ourselves—you'll learn the answers to all your questions in the upcoming chapters.

YOUR NEXT QUESTION IS, WHO ARE WE?

We've been working in the learning and digital product space for the past two decades as both developers and coaches. We've been helping organizations set up and launch dojos since 2014. The examples you'll read about are culled from our experience, although we've changed details to protect the identity and privacy of the companies involved.

Our approach involves solving problems holistically and isn't limited to writing better code and using better technology. It includes focusing on creating better products and fully engaged teams, all while fostering deeper, stickier learning. We believe the challenges to creating great digital products go beyond technology. When we work with teams, we address practices across the entire product development value stream.

A HOLISTIC APPROACH

Teams are faced with a conundrum: they often want to reduce delivery times, improve technical quality, and create products with a better product/market fit, but they must slow down to learn the practices that will improve their product development capability.

The dojo takes a holistic approach, bringing together cross-functional teams and placing them in an immersive learning environment. Teams learn new practices and how these practices tie together. Unlike traditional training where practices are learned in sandbox environments with canned examples, teams learn within the context of doing their real-world work, where constraints come into play. Learning becomes part of what teams do, as opposed to a special event.

THE SIX-WEEK DOJO EXPERIENCE

Joan sought out the director of IT transformation, who put her in touch with us. In our early conversations with Joan and her leadership, we backed her up in her desire for creating a cross-functional or full-stack team—at least for the time they'd be in the dojo. This new team would have all the necessary people to deliver a digital product. We guided Joan to assemble a team that comprised not only developers and testers, but people from the business side of the organization who understood the product being developed, designers, and people from operations.

Although the team members were all employed by the same organization, they had never actually worked together as a unified team. Coming into the dojo was going to be different—the team would work together all day, every day, for the next six weeks.

We began the first day by starting to work with product discovery practices. This surprised them. They had expected the dojo to be another training where they learned about technical practices or focused on process minutiae. The team member from operations couldn't understand why he was being asked to participate in product discovery. The whole team was skeptical about our methods. We asked them to indulge us for a few hours, and if they didn't find the product discovery practices valuable, we'd jump into technical practices.

Within the first hour, the team started a discussion that clarified their understanding of the product needs. For perhaps the first time, the domain experts, engineers, and testers were having a direct conversation with each other. Even the operations person got in on the action. For some of the engineers, it was the first time someone asked them to think about the people using the product instead of coding requirements from a specification. Discrepancies surfaced about expectations for the product they would build over the next six weeks. The team quickly understood the importance of doing discovery and design—together—before jumping into delivery, and everyone could see the impact taking this first step would have on the quality of their product. Needless to say, they found value in what they were learning, so we spent a week on product discovery practices.

We built a product backlog—but in a way that was new for the team. Instead of getting overly focused on creating a list of things to build, we focused on the outcomes they wanted to achieve for their product and the learning they wanted to achieve while they were in the dojo. The team learned how to use story mapping[1] to give additional dimensions to the information. This supported the team's ability to make decisions about their next best investments in delivering value with their product and achieving their learning goals.

At the beginning of the second week, we started on product delivery. The developers learned how to code using test-driven development, the team began learning how to do automated builds and deployments, and the test engineers learned how to automate tests that had previously been exercised manually.

At one point, the developer who'd been on the receiving end of the tester's wrath spun around in her chair to talk to the tester. She said, "Hey, I know we're still working on getting your automated tests to run as part of the build, but that functionality that you've been writing tests for is now deployed in the test environment. You can go ahead and test it."

The tester pulled up his automated test cases, clicked a button, and ran all the test cases. When he saw that one of them was failing, he spun his chair back to the developer and said, "Hey, there's one test failing. I'm not getting the

---

1   To learn more about story mapping, we suggest Jeff Patton, *User Story Mapping: Discover the Whole Story, Build the Right Product* (Sebastopol, CA: O'Reilly, 2014).

expected return values." The developer looked at the test results and said, "I know what's wrong. I can fix that right away." The code was fresh in her mind because she'd just worked on it.

Communication happens in real time in a dojo, and product team members learn how to collaborate effectively with each other. In this situation, the developer went back to the code, fixed it, and fifteen minutes later there was a new build deployed in the test environment. The tester ran the tests, and this time all the tests passed.

Joan smiled as she watched this exchange. Two former adversaries were now on the same team.

During the team's six-week dojo experience, both the leader and the team saw improvements in their delivery times and in the quality of their product. They were able to make these improvements through applying new skills they learned in the dojo in the context of building their own product. Their improvements had a positive impact on the team and on the organization as a whole.

They could finally get the outcomes they had failed to achieve with two-day courses and workshops. Joan was already thinking about bringing her team back into the dojo later in the year to learn how to migrate their services to the cloud.

Would you like to offer your teams a similar experience? You can.

LEARN TO CREATE YOUR OWN DOJO

The world today is increasingly fast-paced and is even more so for anyone who works with digital products. Change is the only constant. Organizations can no longer afford to send their employees to two-day trainings for learning that doesn't stick. They need to become learning organizations, where learning while doing is the norm, not the exception. To that end, organizations are using dojos to offer immersive learning experiences in-house.

In the pages that follow, you'll see how immersive learning in the dojo setting is far more effective than traditional training and coaching. We'll take you through the steps of creating your own dojo and offer guidance on the following topics:

- Aligning learning outcomes with your organization's product strategy and technology direction
- Choosing the practices you will teach
- Setting up the physical space
- Staffing a dojo
- Running six-week dojo experiences and other dojo offerings

- Leveraging a dojo to make improvements across the entire organization

This book is not a typical boring training manual or a treatise on technical practices. It's about creating real-world learning experiences, illustrated with stories and actionable tasks.

The concept of the dojo as an immersive learning and practice space goes back thousands of years in the realms of Buddhism and martial arts. Likewise, immersive learning is not new to the technology space. In the early days of Agile, several organizations offered immersive learning experiences. More recently, the DevOps community has embraced creating learning organizations. In the tech world, the dojo can be the first step for an organization to create a culture of continuous learning and improvement.

The first dojo opened in one company in 2015. Over the course of five years, more than thirty organizations we know of have implemented dojos in one form or another. Ten of them rank in the top one hundred of the Fortune 500. Half of the organizations are listed in the Fortune 500 and Fortune Global 500. They represent a broad range of industries including automakers, airlines, financial services, insurance, healthcare, retail, food and beverage, farm machinery, manufacturing, and telecommunications.

In addition, an informal working group called the Dojo Consortium meets virtually every two weeks and has participation from more than twenty organizations. They share information with each other on topics ranging from getting stakeholder support for creating dojos and hiring coaches to measuring a dojo's impact. We organized the first Dojo Consortium conference in Minneapolis in the spring of 2019. The consortium members have voted to make that a yearly event.

Dojos are investments in your people, your culture, and your organization. Dojos take time, but the results are impactful—happier and more engaged employees, better products, less organizational friction, and more satisfied customers.

You can't just hire your way into these outcomes. You can't hire the best people and put them in a broken system. If you create a dojo, as teams go through the experience, the cracks in your organization will begin to show—and that's an opportunity for your organization to grow and improve. You need to start today to create an environment that helps your teams and your organization learn.

Are you ready to take the first step into the immersive learning experience of a dojo? If so, turn the page. You and your company will be glad you did.

Chapter One

HOW WE LEARN

A single intense, out-of-context classroom event can only get you started in the right direction, at best. You need continuing goals, you need to get feedback to understand your progress, and you need to approach the whole thing far more deliberately than a once-a-year course in a stuffy classroom.

—ANDY HUNT, *PRAGMATIC THINKING AND LEARNING: REFACTORING YOUR WETWARE*

Once upon a time, you learned a trade, maybe through an apprenticeship, and then performed that trade more or less in the same way throughout your professional lifetime. If you wanted to be a blacksmith, you worked alongside a seasoned blacksmith until you could forge iron with a certain mastery. Your blacksmith education ended there. Neither the tools nor the materials changed. You honed your blacksmithing skills by the simple nature of repeating the same movements, but you weren't required to learn new skills.

In most professions today, whether you're a developer writing code for an app, a radiation oncologist treating cancer patients, or a chef cooking dinner for heads of state, you're required to learn how to use new tools as they reach the market and add new skills as practices in your field change.

Even if you manage to keep up with all the changes in technology and the technical skills associated with them, building digital products requires ongoing contact with your customers to stay current with their needs. As it turns out, there are practices for doing that as well. Adopting and implementing these practices helps to ensure your product maintains product/market fit over time.

Learning new tools and skills, then, is a never-ending requirement of modern professions. We must become lifelong learners, and the organizations in which we work must become learning organizations that promote and support ongoing learning.

In its most essential form, the dojo creates an environment where teams become lifelong learners in a learning organization. To understand why this is a more effective way to learn, let's consider why traditional training methods are ineffective.

YOU TRAIN A DOG, YOU TEACH PEOPLE

When you take your dog to a training school, he learns to do things by command: sit, stay, roll over. Training programs for humans often follow the same rote repetition. Humans, however, learn through experience and reflection. Following instructions isn't learning per se, and successfully duplicating steps in some recipe-like format doesn't mean we can reproduce the results on our own. To learn to consider a problem and solve it, we need to understand what's happening when we do the tasks.

Short-term training has a host of problems, but perhaps the most significant is that the training environment is never the same as the real environment (much like dog training, where there are never pesky cats on the training field to distract your dog from a long stay command). In a training sandbox, you're given explicit instructions—do this, do that, do the next thing—and nothing goes wrong. As soon as you return to your desk, you're dealing with constraints in the form of existing legacy code, security issues limiting access to resources, modifications to tools for compliance with governance standards, and a host of other issues. You may understand the mechanics of what was taught in the two-day course, but when you return to your own environment, you can't apply them.

The problems aren't limited to technical training. For example, when you learn product discovery practices in a two-day training, you can grasp the practices, and you may even apply them to new ideas you have for your real-world products. However, the product ideas you work on in these short courses don't have the history of your own products—history filled with attachment to previous decisions, constraints of promises already made, and technical limitations.

More problems occur when you're the only member of your team at the training. You may learn the practices perfectly, but as soon as you return to the team, you quickly run into conflicts with people who haven't attended the training. You may be unable to apply what you've learned. For example, if you're the only one on your team who's attended a test-driven development course, it will be hard to get the full benefits of that practice if your coworkers are committing code without tests.

In our own experience with two-day training events—which, in all transparency, we teach in addition to the dojo model—we've seen that during the course, everyone's excited, understands the concepts, and knows how the new skills will be used when they return to their cubicles. After the training, however, people forget how to use those new skills, or the existing practices create obstacles to adopting the new practices. For this reason, we structure all of our training engagements to include exercises using real-world product development. We include follow-up coaching, so we can address real-world constraints impossible to address in a two-day course.

CERTIFIED DOESN'T MEAN QUALIFIED

Standard training courses often focus on specific branded frameworks or commercial tools. This is so common in the Agile framework space we don't even need to mention the frameworks by name. Examples in the tool space include specific cloud platforms and DevOps tools. Attendees of these courses often receive certifications, sometimes advancing in levels by attending more courses.

Learning frameworks and tools has value, but selling courses and charging for certification tests has become a lucrative money-making industry in and of itself. Most importantly, having the certification doesn't always translate into having the skills the certification implies. Often there is no requirement to demonstrate competency. In other cases, certification requires passing a test; but how valid is a multiple-choice test in proving you know how to use a tool?

Consider driving: to get your driver's license, you don't just play a video game simulation. You have to drive in the real world. Even so, we all have a relative who is "certified" to drive a vehicle, but we wouldn't want to be in the car with them on a wintry night.

LEARNING ALONE IN A TEAM WORLD

Many organizations offer employees access to self-paced, individual training platforms. Employees can access books, video content, and online courses. These platforms have their place, but they're no substitute for whole-team learning. It does no good for a few people on a team to learn a new practice if that practice is not going to be supported by the whole team. In other cases, people spend time learning skills they find interesting, like new languages or frameworks, but those skills may not have a whole lot of value if the team is never going to adopt those languages or frameworks.

In addition, collaborative learning is more effective than individual learning. In *The Accelerated Learning Handbook: A Creative Guide to Designing and Delivering Faster, More Effective Training Programs*,[1] Dave Meier states, "All good learning has a social base. We often learn more by interacting with peers than we learn by any other means. Competition between learners slows learning. Cooperation among learners speeds it. A genuine learning community is always better for learning than a collection of isolated individuals."

Our experience helping teams learn supports these assertions.

---

1   Dave Meier, *The Accelerated Learning Handbook: A Creative Guide to Designing and Delivering Faster, More Effective Training Programs* (New York: McGraw-Hill, 2000), 9.

LEARNING TO RIDE A BIKE

We think we go to school—or a training course—to learn or gain knowledge. We tend to overemphasize metaphors like knowledge transfer, knowledge exchange, and knowledge management. We act as if knowledge can be moved around like any other commodity and that we will gain new knowledge through a simple act of consumption. The truth is, acquiring new knowledge is an active act of creation. Obviously, people with knowledge we don't have can assist us in the knowledge creation process, but they can't simply "give" their knowledge to us.

Remember when you learned to ride a bicycle? You probably saw a parent or older sibling, let's say your sister, on her bicycle, legs moving in circles, maybe laughing or whooping as the breeze cooled her face. You wanted to experience that freedom of movement. Your sister didn't give you a manual on riding a bicycle or stand in front of a dry-erase board and draw a diagram to explain the anatomy of your quads contracting to push your feet down to apply pressure to the pedal to turn the wheel, or the physics behind keeping your balance. She put you on the seat of a two-wheeler and pushed. At first the pedals pushed your feet more than your feet pushed the pedals, but then you got the hang of it. She ran alongside you, holding the back of the seat to help you understand balance. She may have done this many times. Eventually, she let go and you were pedaling and moving forward while the wind cooled your face. She helped you create your own knowledge of how to ride a bike.

That's how humans learn.

There are two kinds of knowledge:

- Explicit knowledge can be written down (or captured in some other form, like video) and stored. When information is categorized, organized for consumption, and stored, it is being made explicit. Someone else can consume it without any direct contact with the person who documented the information. Hopefully, new knowledge will be created through the consumption of that explicit knowledge.
- Tacit knowledge, on the other hand, is knowledge we've acquired through experience and practice and is difficult or maybe even impossible to document. It is highly contextual. We may not even be 100 percent conscious of having it until someone asks us a question or a situation requires us to access it. Tacit knowledge shows up as intuition, gut feelings, and experience that tells you the decisions to make. Sharing tacit knowledge requires feedback loops, dialogue, answering questions, and validation that the person on the receiving end "gets it."

In the world of technology, there are a lot of things that

can be made explicit: we can share code examples, write tutorials, and document patterns for solutions to commonly recurring problems. A mistake that organizations often make is believing everything can be made explicit and that getting teams up to speed on the latest and greatest skills is simply a matter of giving people access to the right books or learning platforms, that is, the right forms of explicit knowledge. Organizations underestimate the amount of person-to-person contact needed to foster knowledge creation through the exchange of tacit knowledge. They also underestimate the amount of time needed for tacit knowledge exchange.

If this seems too theoretical or like too much of a straw man argument, ask yourself these questions:

- How many times has your organization sent one or two people to a training event or a conference with the idea that they would document what they learned and share that knowledge with the rest of their team and the organization?
- How effective has that been in helping the team adopt new skills or practices?

Organizations need to create holistic, immersive learning environments that balance explicit and tacit learning.

HOLISTIC LEARNING

The product development value stream comprises everything that happens during the product creation life cycle. It begins when someone recognizes an opportunity or a problem and has an idea for a product. The idea is refined during product discovery, gets developed, and is ultimately delivered to the customer in some form, where it provides value. The organization that creates the product captures analytical data about the product's usage, creating a feedback loop that flows into product discovery, so they can continue to improve the product and provide value to the customer. Clearly, a series of activities, events, and processes have to happen to take the product from idea to production, and there are various practices that address different segments of the value stream.

In many organizations, different people who aren't part of the same team work in isolation from each other. They work through different practices in different segments of the value stream. There is weak collaboration between them. Sometimes people working on building the product have no idea why they are working on particular features or capabilities. They are simply "coding to the spec." By the time we get to the people automating deployments with tools, we've lost all connection with the value a particular feature is supposed to provide to the customer.

What does this have to do with learning? A lot.

Training courses typically address small segments of the value stream. One short workshop might focus on product discovery, which is an early segment of the value stream; another might focus on one of the Agile frameworks, which typically address the delivery segment of the value stream.

You might send your domain experts and designers to a product discovery course, while you send your delivery team to an Agile framework course. Attendees of the product discovery course might learn new techniques for writing stories, like story mapping. People in the Agile framework course may be taught to write stories following the "as a (blank), I can (blank), so that (blank)" format. When the people who attended the product discovery course deliver their story maps to the delivery team, friction occurs. The delivery team may insist on rewriting the stories in the format they were taught. (We've seen this exact scenario play out multiple times.)

You've got two groups trying to learn how to do their jobs better and collaborate together, but they're learning from different sources, different philosophies, and different value systems. They get bogged down in the mechanics and the differences in the way they've been taught as opposed to learning how to optimize the flow of work to deliver value to their customers. Ironically, the solution employed to address discrepancies like this in many cases is to add more steps to the process, disconnecting people even further.

When teams come into the dojo, we teach them how to holistically address the entire value stream. The team within the dojo becomes larger because it encompasses the whole product development community and isn't limited to developers or the product discovery team. We aim to build overlapping perspectives and skillsets at multiple points on the value stream, so the entire product community begins to see how the pieces fit together to create products with better product/market fit.

LEARNING THAT STICKS

Ancient Greeks developed mnemonic devices to remember long series of words or numbers, and still today, people demonstrate superhuman memorization skills to earn a listing in the *Guinness World Records* book or so they can compete in World Memory Championships. But what about the rest of us? How does the average person learn and retain facts or skills, especially in a time when distractions and information overload are the norm rather than the exception?

Researchers have been trying to harness the secret to a better memory for centuries. In 1885, Hermann Ebbinghaus developed the Ebbinghaus forgetting curve theory, which uses a mathematical formula to calculate how long we retain a fact or skill in relation to how much time has passed since we learned the fact or skill. The curve is steeper than we'd like it to be:

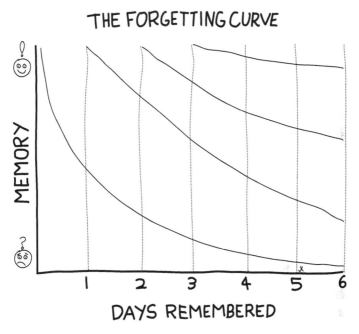

THE FORGETTING CURVE

We forget more easily than we might think we do.

Modern research estimates we forget 90 percent of what we learn in a standard classroom setup in the first month after it's been learned—some even cite the first week. Ebbinghaus was way ahead of them. His research showed that the quality of our retention is based on two things: repetition (particularly spaced repetition) and the quality of the representation of the memory itself.

Learning in the dojo model is effective in part because it addresses both of these concerns.

Repetition is the name of the game in the dojo. Teams work in two-and-a-half-day sprints, which provide opportunities to work with new practices multiple times.

Representation of the memory itself refers to how you store the information in your mind. The quality of the memory representation improves when the memory is important to you and when you're able to create strong associations with the concepts you're learning. In the dojo, if you're learning skills in the context of the work that you have to do every day, you will create stronger associations than you would when learning sandbox exercises in a training course that has nothing to do with your daily work. The dojo creates an ideal environment for learning that sticks, that is, learning that people will remember.

CONTINUOUS LEARNING

A lot of organizations say learning is important. They budget time and funding for learning, but they also treat learning as a separate event that takes place outside the normal workday. The truth is, especially in IT, learning is given a lot of lip service and is only important when the team isn't busy—which is never.

When organizations build a dojo, they are making an investment in learning and acknowledging that learning can't be limited to one-off, separate events. When teams come into the dojo, the myth of learning being a separate event is quickly exposed. Teams discover that learning is an ongoing and continuous effort that happens throughout the entire value stream. They learn to acknowledge what they don't know and work on solving problems together, growing new skills along the way.

Teams leave the dojo knowing how to apply this continuous learning and improvement as they continue to work outside the dojo—they don't get that from traditional approaches to training, workshops, or courses.

TRADITIONAL TRAINING	DOJO
Practices are taught with predefined exercises completed, step-by-step, in clean sandbox environments.	Practices are taught while doing product development in the organization's environments subject to real-world constraints and limitations.
Learning is focused on the individual. There is a high risk of new skills not being adopted by the whole team.	Whole teams learn practices together, developing shared understanding and values. This supports long-term adoption of new practices and skills.
There is limited time for assessment, questions, and feedback required for tacit knowledge exchange.	Time for assessment, questions, and feedback is a core part of the dojo model. Conscious attention is paid to tacit knowledge exchange.
A single set of practices related to one skill is taught in isolation without providing context of how those practices fit into the bigger picture.	Practices related to multiple skills applying to the entire product development value stream are taught holistically. Learners understand how the practices are interrelated.
Exercises are done in a step-by-step progression with little to no repetition or practice. There is a high risk of quickly forgetting new information.	Repeated practice and application of new practices leads to long-term skill improvement, that is, learning that sticks.
Learning is a one-off, special event. Learning is viewed as being separate and distinct from daily work.	Learning and continuous improvement become part of a team's daily work. The organization becomes a learning organization.

Today, the complex products organizations develop require a high level of collaboration and a mindset of continuous learning. We can agree that learning is individual—you have to create new knowledge for yourself. In the context of individual learning, however, a collaborative space encourages sharing ideas and helping each other if we get stuck.

A dojo fills the need for a collaborative learning environment. A huge portion of working and learning in the dojo happens because we're supporting each other's learning and improving how we collaborate. We walk through an overview of the dojo experience in chapter 2 and then we'll unpack each part fully in the chapters that follow.

PRACTICES, SKILLS, AND OFFERINGS

We use the terms "practices," "skills," and "offerings" throughout this book. It's worth clarifying the meaning behind these terms, at least in the context of how we use them when we're talking about dojos.

Practices are specific techniques or processes teams learn to increase their skills. For example, test-driven development is a practice that helps teams increase their software design skills. Prototyping and customer interviews are practices that help teams increase their product discovery skills.

We think of offerings as the products your dojo offers. The "standard" offering we describe in this book is the six-week dojo experience where improvements to specific skills and related practices are defined on a team-by-team basis. Another offering we've delivered in dojos is a week-long design sprint focused on improving product discovery skills and related practices. As you consider creating offerings for your dojo, you'll want to consider what skills teams want to improve and what practices will help them improve those skills.

Chapter Two

_____

THE DOJO EXPERIENCE

I have been impressed with the urgency of doing. Knowing is not enough; we must apply. Being willing is not enough; we must do.

—LEONARDO DA VINCI

The dojo is about learning by doing, first and foremost. Dojos don't have a standard curriculum. Teams work on gaining skills by learning and applying new practices to their real-world work. Whole teams learn new practices together and they learn them in the context of the constraints and limitations that exist within their organization.

Why do we do it this way?

LEARNING BY DOING

Teams often get bogged down in the decision-making process around what they should do next. There's a never-ending list of changes they could make to improve the product and ideas for technical improvements, whether the ideas are for cleaning up existing code or implementing entirely new technology. Often, teams become paralyzed while considering what to do next. When considering any change, they get bogged down thinking about all the possible ways things could go wrong before they begin to try different solutions. In the dojo, we encourage them to experiment and learn from doing the work.

One team in a dojo was struggling with deciding which way to implement an address lookup. There were plenty of third-party map tools they could leverage, but they didn't understand how each tool would affect the product. They didn't understand the technology. The team started going down a rabbit hole, discussing all the ways they could use the map tools. We said, "Let's just try one example with one tool, and then after we've done it, let's talk about what we've learned." The team spent an hour trying one of the map tools for the address lookup. Afterward, they discussed what they learned about the tool, the problem space, and how well the tool worked for the address lookup. The next time a problem came up, they started to spin around all of the possibilities for solving it until somebody on the team said, "Why don't we just pick an approach, try an example, and see what we learn."

Another group was working on a product to keep store inventory up-to-date. There are many ways to update an inventory, and the group was, again, stuck in the decision-making process. Instead of researching the problem for weeks and going off on tangents, they were able to frame up what they wanted to learn about the problem. Then, they went through the learning together, shared what they learned with their leaders, and made a decision about how they were going to keep inventory up-to-date. The learning cycle was faster, because they intentionally chose to learn by doing. They owned their learning.

These events happen all the time while teams are building products, but seldom do they take the time to reflect upon what is happening, what is being learned. During a dojo experience, teams learn practices and skills and—just as importantly—they learn how to learn.

OVERVIEW OF THE DOJO FLOW
THE INTAKE PROCESS

The life cycle of a dojo experience begins with the intake process, which we fully describe in chapters 6 and 7. The dojo staff, who we introduce in chapter 5, conduct the intake process, comprising the overview, consult, and chartering.

Overview

A person or a team will discover the dojo and be curious to learn what it is. They may walk past the dojo space and ask, "What is this place?" Or they might read about it in a company newsletter and seek out more information. Initial interest could come from a whole team, a single person on a team, or a leader higher up in the organization who leads multiple teams.

The overview is the first contact between the dojo and an interested party.

The first questions the dojo staff are asked are usually "What is a dojo?" and "How does it work?" The dojo staff answer these questions and start learning about the interested party. The conversation is light and informal, with the interested party getting a general understanding of the dojo and the dojo staff getting a general understanding of the interested party. The primary goal of the dojo staff is to steer the contact toward a consultation, or consult.

Consult

The purpose of the consult is to teach a team what a dojo is and to set expectations with a team around how the dojo works should they decide to sign up for a dojo experience. Team managers need to understand that the team will need time to learn. Managers need to make sure space is created in the team's schedule for the learning to happen. The dojo staff needs to understand what the team wants to learn, so they can help the team be successful. The goals of the consult are for the team members to understand the expectations of the dojo, to foster interest in learning together, and for the dojo staff to learn about the team's high-level learning goals.

The consult may be informal, or the dojo staff can prepare a presentation explaining what the dojo is and how it works. It's also a good idea to share experiences and results of teams who have been through the dojo. Sometimes, in the first consult leaders will want to have a conversation with the dojo staff without their team, and that's fine. It's important, however, that the whole team meets with the dojo staff in a second consult meeting. When the leader is ready to bring the whole team in for a consultation, it's a good sign that they're leaning toward committing to a dojo experience.

Assuming the team goes through the consult and decides to continue, the next step is chartering.

Chartering

Chartering (chapter 7) is a half-day activity scheduled to take place one to two weeks before the six-week dojo experience begins. Chartering can lead to the discovery of items that need to be addressed prior to a team starting in the dojo, which is why we charter at least a week before the team begins. The team meets with the coaches from the dojo staff to build a shared understanding of what success looks like for the team over the course of the six weeks. They establish a defined list of goals; if they hit all those goals, everyone would be really happy that they came to the dojo.

The team talks about what practices they want to learn and how learning those practices will help them. For example, a team could say, "By learning to automate our deployments, we expect to remove errors from the deployment process and spend less time trouble-shooting why a deployment isn't working as expected." In chartering, we want to make sure we're connecting learning goals with outcomes that will help teams deliver better products.

THE SIX-WEEK EXPERIENCE

As we've described, this book is focused primarily on the "standard" dojo offering, where teams go into a dojo for six weeks. A typical day involves learning tools and practices and applying them to product development. Teams work in two-and-a-half-day sprints. Chapter 8 outlines the cadence of the six-week experience.

Over the course of the dojo experience, the team will have twelve sprints in which they repeatedly practice what they learn. For example, a team might be new to TDD (test-driven development). The first test a team writes might be easy—they could choose a simple test without any dependencies on other systems. They understand the flow of writing the test, getting it to pass, and refactoring the code to make quality improvements. However, it's still shallow learning because it was just one test, and an easy one at that. Just because they understand the mechanics of writing the test doesn't mean they know how to apply those mechanics to a more complex scenario. The team writes another test; the product context is the same, but the way they need to test changes. Perhaps the first test was a happy path scenario with no external dependencies, and this next test has an error and one external dependency, like an alerting system. The concept of testing is repeated, but the approach changes. Deep mastery occurs through repeating the practice in different scenarios, learning how to make adjustments along the way. The multiple small sprints provide opportunities for practice and repetition, fostering deeper learning and stickiness—the retention of that learning.

Smaller sprints also encourage teams to reflect on how they are learning together, something they often neglect. Although retrospectives are a fundamental aspect of Agile methodologies, reflecting on learning is often a new concept for teams. The idea is to reflect on how well the team is meeting its learning goals and to see if the team would like to try anything different. Teams pause at the end of a sprint and ask, "What would we like to try differently to foster learning during the next sprint? What do we expect will happen if we make this change?" We ask the team to think of ways that they would know the change was a good idea—to give an example of how they would measure the impact of the change, even if it's subjectively. In this way, the dojo is fostering intentional learning and continuous improvement. Repeating the retrospective frequently within the dojo makes it a habit the team takes back to their normal work environment.

Learning in a dojo happens through experience. Teams revisit their goals often during the six weeks. They think about whether they're learning the right things and whether or not what they're learning is helping them make a better product.

POST-DOJO

When the team concludes the six-week experience, the dojo staff conducts exit interviews to assess how well the experience went for the team. Based on those interviews, they develop a transition plan to ensure that the new practices, the new style of working, and the focus on continuous learning and improvement continue when the team returns to their normal work environment.

Chapter 9 fully discusses post-dojo activities.

WHAT MAKES A DOJO A DOJO?

Dojos are gaining enough notoriety that companies are starting to rebrand existing products as dojos. Products that were previously called "labs" now have the word "dojo" in their name. What looks like standard Agile coaching that's been around for years is now being called a dojo. More and more consulting firms are offering dojo-related services. We think this is great—assuming that what's being called a dojo is indeed a dojo. Unfortunately, in some cases it may just be an attempt to cash in on a good idea.

(NOTE: we are not referring to the use of the term "coding dojos" here. Coding dojos have been around far longer than the dojo model we describe in this book. The two share common values around deliberate practice, group learning, and repetition when learning new techniques and practices. For those interested in learning more about coding dojos, Emily Bache's book *The Coding Dojo Handbook* is a great reference.)

We are often asked "What makes a dojo a dojo?" Dojos are pragmatic by design. Organizations create dojos to meet the needs of their teams where they are at and to teach teams skills that will help them deliver better products in their specific markets. This may result in the creation of dojos that vary significantly from organization to organization.

Here is what we see as being negotiable and nonnegotiable principles for calling something a dojo.

Nonnegotiable

- Learning over delivery
- Whole-team learning
- Spaced repetition and opportunity for repeated practice
- Skilled coaching
- Learning in context of real-world work
- Collaborative peer-to-peer learning
- Safe-to-fail learning (in small increments)

Negotiable (assuming nonnegotiable principles are met)

- Offerings
- Duration of offerings
- Skills and practices learned
- The physical space

When starting your dojo, we suggest you start with the six-week offering. You can add additional offerings once you've established the six-week offering. However, providing too many offerings of differing durations could be confusing for potential teams.

Over time, your dojo will become established as a known product within your organization. You will learn from your experiences with teams. You may discover there's an opportunity to address specific skills or problems with offerings of shorter durations. Some dojos have created a one-week offering focusing heavily on product discovery with user research and prototyping. Other dojos have created short two- or three-day experiences where teams can come in to learn a specific technology, like Kubernetes. Another dojo even created an extended offering lasting ten weeks where people brand-new to technology learned how to write code and build products! All great ideas...but not right off the bat. Early on, make it easy for your customers to say "yes" to your product by limiting your offerings.

A SAFE SPACE TO LEARN

Going back to the Ebbinghaus curve—without the opportunity for practice and repetition, learning will not stick. Often, skill growth is just expected to happen while people are doing their work. There's no space in the schedule for the learning to occur. And there's absolutely no room for failure—even on a small scale and even though we often learn more from our failures than from our successes. In most organizations, teams simply can't ever be wrong.

The ability to innovate is lost when there's no room for failure or learning. People become conservative, falling back to what they already know instead of trying to apply new ideas. Or, when they have to implement new technologies, they'll do it without really understanding them. Asking people to adopt new practices and acquire new skills without giving them time to learn those new practices and skills results in poor quality products. By its nature, a dojo becomes a space where applying new practices and skills has a lower emotional and financial risk. In the following chapters, we explain how to choose the practices you'll offer, how to set up the space, and who will run your dojo. We then walk you through the steps for running your own dojo experience.

Chapter Three

CHOOSING THE PRACTICES YOU WILL TEACH

You have brains in your head. You have feet in your shoes. You can steer yourself any direction you choose. You're on your own. And you know what you know. And YOU are the one who'll decide where to go.

—DR. SEUSS, *OH, THE PLACES YOU'LL GO!*

Efficiency and effectiveness. Two simple words, yet the one we choose to focus on drives so much of our organizational behavior.

Efficiency is about minimizing the amount of time and effort it takes to get work done. In organizations aiming for efficiency, the focus is on ensuring everyone is allocated to 100 percent of their capacity—even if that means assigning them to multiple efforts at the same time. The primary metrics the organization captures ensure utilization goals are met.

Effectiveness, on the other hand, focuses on getting work done that will have the right impacts and achieve desired outcomes. Metrics in organizations focused on being effective measure the level of impact and how well the organization is achieving those outcomes. Often, the most effective teams and organizations might not look very efficient.

What does this have to do with a dojo and choosing the practices you will teach?

Everything.

If your organization repeatedly develops high-quality products with great product/market fit that delight your customers, by all means focus on efficiency. But that's not the reality for most organizations. And focusing solely on being more efficient when you're delivering products with quality problems or that continually miss the mark with your customers may not lead to the outcomes you're hoping to achieve.

Dojos have the most impact when organizations use them to create more effective product development teams.

ALIGNING WITH STRATEGY

As you create a dojo, you want to understand your organization's strategic direction and the outcomes it's trying to achieve. You want to offer teams the opportunity to learn practices and skills that will help them develop products in line with the organization's goals. For example, your organization's strategic direction might be to migrate workloads to the cloud to improve time to market and reduce costs. Based upon these goals, your dojo could help teams learn cloud-native development, teaching skills like the twelve-factor app methodology, chaos engineering, and distributed systems monitoring. Another organization might have a strategic direction of improving product/market fit. Their dojo could teach practices around customer research, right-fidelity prototyping, and A/B testing.

The dojo is a product in its own right. You want to do product discovery and ideation on the dojo before you build and run the dojo. At first, think about the following questions to get on the right track:

- Why are you creating a dojo?
- What pain points do you want to solve for?
- What opportunities are you hoping to take advantage of?
- What improvements are you hoping to make?
- How will you know if you are successful?

You might find yourself answering the questions with statements such as "We want better development practices." Great. If you had better development practices, what results would you get? Your answer might be that you'd have fewer defects and fewer unexpected issues from changes to your system components that you thought were isolated from each other.

Once you identify pain points and opportunities, you can use them to help you identify which practices your dojo will help teams learn.

Organizations become effective when people understand the full product development value stream and how their work contributes to developing great products. In the dojo, they learn delivery practices that help them improve the technical quality of their products. They learn product discovery practices that help them improve their chances of developing products with better product/market fit. And they learn how to reduce development cycle times by reducing queues and eliminating real sources of waste in the value stream instead of being solely focused on the "waste" of an individual having slack time in their schedule.

The product development value stream looks at the flow of value delivery within your organization. It starts with an idea for a product addressing a customer need or taking advantage of an opportunity and ends when the customer is deriving value from the delivered product. (This, of course, assumes the product was deployed in such a way that usage can be monitored, practices like A/B testing are used, and there is direct interaction with the customer to ensure they are deriving value.)

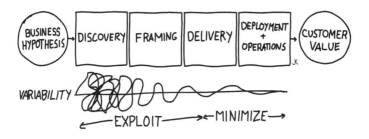

Simplified view of the product development value stream

Those familiar with value stream mapping will notice the above image doesn't include details on the individual processes or steps, cycle times, data about how well processes are done, or the people involved in each step. However, we find this simple view helpful to start discussions around defining practices your dojo will support. If your organization has gone through an exercise to document your product development value stream in detail, by all means use your own value stream to drive the conversation.

The four broad sections of our product development value stream include the following:

- Discovery: Product discovery is a process used to determine whether a product idea is worth building or not. It's used to explore, validate, and develop product ideas. It consists of practices including product canvases, personas, story maps, customer interviews, and right-fidelity prototyping.
- Framing: Product framing is a set of techniques used to "frame up" delivery, that is, how are we going to go about building our product? It includes practices like domain-driven design, architecture patterns, and refining story maps with journeys and slices.
- Delivery: Product delivery includes all the practices we use to deliver our product. There is a large set of practices here. Examples include test-driven development, continuous integration, trunk-based development, and design patterns. It also includes Agile and Lean process practices.
- Deployment and Operations: Deployment and operations include all the practices used to deploy and operate products in development, testing, and production environments. Example practices include infrastructure setup automation, automated deployments, monitoring, patching, and incident response. Many of the DevOps practices apply to this part of the value stream.

As you look at this simplified view of a product development value stream, it might already be triggering ideas for practices you'd like to support in your dojo. In many organizations we work with, there is little or no focus on product discovery. Either discovery is viewed as someone else's job or ideas move straight from inception to defining requirements and delivery without ever being vetted by customers. If this is true for your organization, you may be thinking it would be a good idea to support product discovery practices. We'd agree.

The product development value stream may also be triggering ideas about practices to address current pain points in your organization. For example, you might have fragile, unstable development and testing environments, so you might decide to teach practices around environment setup and infrastructure automation. Your pain points may be related to high defect counts in production code. You could choose to teach practices like test-driven development and behavior-driven development or, more generally, test automation.

As you are coming up with ideas for what practices you'll teach, list them under the appropriate segment of the product development value stream.

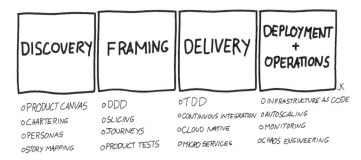

Practices associated with the corresponding segment of the value stream

At this point, you are not committing to offering any of these practices. You're simply brainstorming about practices you might offer and you're considering how those practices could address opportunities for improvement and known pain points in your current product development efforts.

This is a very simple view of practices associated with different segments of the product development value stream. But these practices are never really applicable to only one segment of the value stream. Some practices can be used in multiple segments of the value stream. Some practices help with the transition from one segment of the value stream to the next. Consider DevOps, for example. DevOps practices intentionally focus on improving the product development value stream by improving the transition between delivery and deployment and operations. (It might even be more accurate to say DevOps aims to remove the boundary between delivery and deployment and operations.)

More importantly, different practices from different segments of the value stream are interrelated. Adding or improving practices in the early segments of the value stream can have a significant impact on subsequent segments of the value stream.

An example will illustrate this point.

Many organizations are currently implementing microservice architectures. Consequently, many organizations we work with want to include practices around building microservices during the delivery segment of the product development value stream. There's an obvious link to learning how to automate infrastructure setup and deployment to support a microservice architecture.

What's not so obvious is the amount of skill that needs to be developed to be able to correctly define the boundaries between microservices. Organizations unfortunately sometimes replace big balls of mud (monolithic systems with tight coupling between components) with distributed little balls of mud (tightly coupled microservices). One common anti-pattern is creating microservices for each high-level entity and creating simple CRUD (create, read, update, delete) operations for each microservice. This happens when organizations get more focused on the technical aspects of microservice implementation and don't pay enough attention to microservice design.

One approach to microservice design is to use domain-driven design (DDD), a set of patterns and techniques for managing complexity in software development by designing systems built on models based on a strong understanding of the problem domain. DDD provides techniques for defining appropriate boundaries around microservices. In turn, adopting DDD practices benefits greatly from product discovery practices like product canvases, personas, and story mapping—practices that will help you build up a strong understanding of the problem domain.

Finally, there are practices that will help you understand how well your microservices are working. Obvious practices include things like logging and monitoring to see how well the services are working in production. Less obvious are practices like A/B testing, which will show you how well your microservices are working from a product perspective. Is the customer even using them?

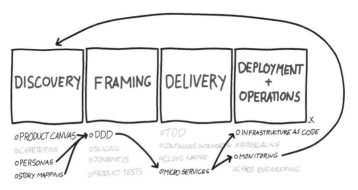

Practices in different parts of the value stream affect each other.

Putting it all together, we can see how these practices along the entire product development value stream support and depend upon each other.

FOCUSING ON PART OF THE VALUE STREAM

Knowing all of the things you could teach and recognizing the interdependencies between them, how will you choose? Will you offer all the practices you identified or only some of them? Will you begin with fewer practices and then add more as you grow? The more practices you offer, the broader your impact. We'd encourage you to offer a broad set of practices, covering as much of the product development value stream as you are capable of covering.

Some organizations want to focus on the right side of the value stream—delivery, monitoring, and operations—because that is where the immediate pain is felt. They define their problems as high defect rates, long deployment times, and customer complaints about system outages. However, these problems often result from products being developed without organizations having a shared understanding of the customers' needs or properly vetting ideas for products. Problems manifest toward the end of the value stream, but the source is at the beginning. That's not to say you can't begin by offering practices on the far right of the value stream, but you're likely to have greater impact if you also offer practices that are further upstream, to the left. When you start with product discovery practices, the resulting shared understanding of the problem makes practices like automated testing and automated deployment easier.

Another reason dojos often start by focusing on practices on the right side of the value stream is because they're commonly started by people in IT who manage that part of the value stream. In some organizations, DevOps is intended to break down the wall between development and operations; however, there's still a wall between the business and IT. We've spent the last twenty years coaching organizations to break down that wall. We want to see IT shift from fulfilling orders from the business to becoming a partner in the product creation itself. Everyone involved in the value stream should be able to define and influence the ideas for what the product could be.

This division between IT and the business becomes evident when you begin having conversations about practices to include as part of a dojo. While our initial conversations often take place with IT, we'll ask if there are business partners and stakeholders that could participate in the conversation. The dojo can be a powerful tool for creating alignment between IT and the business. That alignment can begin as the dojo is being defined.

Maybe you've been in this industry for a while, as we have. When we started our careers, our involvement in projects usually began with a project kickoff meeting. Another group of people had already done enough definition of the product to get funding approved, and the expected return on investment was already established. We were part of a team who would do the detailed requirements, build the product, verify it worked correctly, and then hand it off to another group of people who would deploy it and ensure it was operating correctly in production. In short, we only had responsibility for a small segment of the product development value stream.

Over time, our approach to developing products has changed. Instead of having separate teams handle different segments of the value stream, we're working with organizations to build product communities that address the value stream holistically. This often involves redefining the concept of what a team is and including people with different skillsets. When we work with teams in a dojo, we're often extending the teams' responsibilities for product development across the entire product development value stream.

In our view, "Agile transformations" are no longer sufficient to enable organizations to compete in today's markets. Traditionally, "Agile" focuses on a subsegment of the product development value stream. (Some might argue this point, but the fact that "DevOps" exists as something apart from "Agile" supports our view.) Forward-thinking organizations are now looking at transformations to help them align product development to the entire value stream. These efforts come under various labels, including "project to product transformation," "moving to product," or "adopting a product model." Whatever you might call the approach, a dojo is a powerful enabler for realigning the organization toward optimizing the entire product development value stream.

INTENTIONAL BOUNDARIES

When you choose the practices you will teach, set boundaries for the teams coming in about what you will and won't teach. You can only coach and teach what you know. Don't tell a team you'll teach a practice if you don't have a coach with the skills necessary to teach that practice.

We've run into situations where a team wants to learn practices supported by the dojo but also wants to learn something outside of that core set of practices—outside the established boundaries. One organization we worked with started their dojo focused on automated infrastructure setup and deployments. A team that came into the dojo wanted to get better at testing. The dojo manager pulled in a few people from outside the dojo to help the team learn better testing practices. While the people who came in to help had excellent testing skills themselves, they lacked context about what the team was trying to accomplish—both from a learning perspective and from a product development perspective. In addition, they hadn't ever coached before. They demonstrated a few testing practices and then left the dojo. Ultimately, the team gained little from the experience.

When a team requests help with a practice that's outside the boundaries of what you currently support, you may be better off simply telling the team no, you're not able to help them with that practice.

Most organizations that launch dojos are already doing some form of Agile or Lean process outside the dojo. If they're doing Scrum, they'll probably use Scrum inside the dojo. If they're doing SAFe, they might use SAFe. If they're doing Kanban, they might use Kanban. The important thing is to be clear about the process that will be used inside the dojo.

It's likely the practices your dojo helps teams learn will include practices from an Agile or Lean process. Dojos have been effective at helping teams learn and improve these practices—even when teams coming into a dojo claim to already know how to "do Agile."

Choose a process that makes sense for your organization

and supports learning. Communicate that process with teams coming into the dojo. Help them understand how the process in the dojo will be different than their normal process. We cover this in more detail in chapter 8.

MEASURING LEARNING

In the past, there was so much room for improvement, simply bringing teams in to increase skills in a few practices was enough to make everyone happy. Today, people want to measure the outcomes and impact of the dojo more precisely.

When considering measuring learning, focus on two key elements:

- The impact of the learning: how is the learning improving the product development value stream?
- Identifying the stickiness of the learning: after teams leave the dojo, how well are the new practices retained and leveraged by the team?

The impact of the learning is framed by the larger goals of the dojo. For instance, if the main purpose of the dojo is to reduce feature-delivery cycle time, then the skills taught in the dojo will focus on that measurement. When a team comes in, we would discuss their cycle time with them, the challenges they have around it, and what they can learn to improve upon it. This may include skills like story mapping and story decomposition, test-driven development, and continuous integration practices.

We're still faced with the question of what specific metrics we'll capture to measure learning in a dojo. Defining appropriate metrics for a dojo is a recurring topic in our blog posts and podcasts and will likely continue to be so for some time.[1]

In general, we group metrics into three categories:

- Organizational reach metrics are simple numbers showing the number of interactions the dojo has with different levels of the organization. While these metrics don't equate to impact, they can be leading indicators for the impact the dojo will have on the organization. These metrics may include the following:
  - Number of teams completing a dojo offering
  - Total number of attendees
  - Number of programs (portfolios) that have had a team complete a dojo offering
- Directional/team-based improvements look at the

---

1   "Measuring Impact in the Dojo," *Dojo and Co.* (blog), November 19, 2017, https://www.
    dojoandco.com/blog/2017/11/20/measuring-impact-in-the-dojo; "Dojo Metrics: Moving from
    What Is Easy to Capture to What Matters," *Dojo and Co.* (blog), November 22, 2017, https://
    www.dojoandco.com/blog/2017/11/9/metrics-moving-from-what-is-easy-to-what-matters;
    Dojo and Co. (podcast),https://www.dojoandco.com/podcast.

directional impact of learning in the dojo and how that learning impacts teams. Metrics may include:

- Number of automated tests
- SQALE code quality index
- Percentage reduction in defects
- Cycle time reduction to deliver a product increment
- Velocity/story count (with the obvious caveat that these can be easily gamed)

· Impact/economic improvements on the organization. These metrics answer the question "Is this initiative having a positive economic impact on the organization?" Sample metrics include:

- Increase in sales conversion
- Cycle time reduction for a delivery with impact (not just delivery, but a delivery that mattered)
- Systematic cost reductions (not silo optimizations that may have detrimental effects in other areas)
- Savings resulting from killing bad product ideas early in the discovery/delivery cycle

This last measurement category is both the hardest and the most important to define and capture. If you've clearly defined the outcomes you want your dojo to help your organization achieve, measurements become easier to define.

DO THIS

You are about to start your dojo and you're deciding what practices to teach. Do the following with the group of people supporting the dojo (coaches, admins, leadership, etc.):

- Visualize your value stream (use the sample in this book as a starting point).
- For the various parts of your value stream, identify practices that could be taught in your dojo.
- Add visualizations that show relationships between those practices. What practices reinforce and support other practices?
- Define the impact you want the dojo to have on the organization.
- Identify what part(s) of the value stream you need to focus on to get that impact. Define boundaries that show what practices you will teach and what practices you will not support.
- Can you teach the practices necessary in the identified areas of the value stream? If so, great! If not, what will you do about it? Will you bring in external help or will you narrow your focus?
- Select a set of practices to support in your dojo.
- Define how you will measure the impact of the dojo.

When you begin thinking about the practices you'll support in your dojo, chances are a few things will come immediately to mind. Those practices are likely spot-on, but we encourage you to dig deeper and expand the practices to include more segments along the product development value stream. Look at the current state of how your teams work today and visualize the future state. What are they going to be capable of in the future to achieve desired outcomes? What set of practices will take them from where they are today to where you want them to be?

Chapter Four

———

THE DOJO SPACE

Imagine. What if our physical workspaces—the specific arrangements of walls and halls, sizes and shapes of rooms— were actually making us smarter or duller, enabling or disabling our individual and collective ability to think? What if a more astute crafting of professional habitats led to a greater ease in dealing with current tasks and a more adept foreshadowing of future ones? What if clever digs allowed us to learn more readily, learn from others, and help others learn? They can. This is the grand story I want to tell.

—JENNY QUILLIEN, *CLEVER DIGS: HOW WORKSPACES CAN ENABLE THOUGHT*

A team walked into a dojo for the first time and murmured to each other:

"This space is so different than our normal space."

"It feels like it's a startup."

"It feels like we're starting up the learning journey."

A dojo space is *supposed* to feel different than a standard working environment. Having a separate physical space demarcates the dojo as something different from the normal day-to-day work. It helps establish the disruptive, curious learning mindset right from the get-go. The social learning environment creates a different energy than the typical environment of heads-down day-to-day delivery. A cool vibe develops in the dojo space when multiple teams go through the learning process together.

There are science and design principles behind creating workspaces and learning spaces. Certain work environments foster more creative and innovative thinking, as well as better teamwork. In her book *Clever Digs: How Workspaces Can Enable Thought*,[1] Jenny Quillien writes:

The Organizational Learning Paradigm

We turn, for immediate inspiration, to the research, reflection, and practice carried out within what is called the organizational learning paradigm. Not mainstream in managerial literature but growing stronger by the day—and

---

1   Jenny Quillien, *Clever Digs: How Workspaces Can Enable Thought* (Ames, IA: Culicidae Press, 2012), 69-71.

these folks have, for a number of years now, been pleading for an architecture "for the learning organization."

Pioneers include Peter Senge—learning is not a technique but a discipline, a continuing practice as is, say, meditation or aikido; Donald Schön—the reflective practitioner eschews tidy problems for the swamp of the ill-defined and difficult ones; Chris Argyris—managers must escape their self-made webs of "skilled incompetence" and pony up to hard truths; Ikujiro Nonaka—managers need to foreground the collectively held tacit knowledge; and Karl Weick—the future is about sense-making, amplifying weak signals and, through an iterative process of discovery, sussing out the forward-looking contexts in which such signals make sense.

Learning—to pick up again the theme of matching malleabilities between the physical and human realms—calls for the range of accommodating spaces subsumed in the activities pointed to by our pioneers: places of retreat for disciplined thoughtfulness, quiet corners for substantive reflectivity and conversation, privacy and time for honest confrontation, supporting tools for collaboration and discovery.

Most of these demands are not difficult in any architectural sense, but without hospitable places these learning activities are unlikely to happen. The desired malleability of physical space frequently relies upon a theatrical mentality which smiles upon changeable props, flexible structures, drop ceilings and raised floors for pipes and wires, movable walls and ecologies of adaptable niches. When physical malleability facilitates social interactions, such as double-looping or reiteratively working out a hunch, a mirroring human (cognitive and emotional) malleability is more likely to surface.

Anyone responsible for designing a dojo space would be well served by reading *Clever Digs* in its entirety.

There's intentionality behind designing a learning space like a dojo—an intentionality that holds true for any space. Think about an art studio, a church, or a dance hall; when you walk in you understand the purpose of the place. The act of going into a different physical environment triggers emotions and reactions in us. When a team walks into the dojo, you want them to think "This place is different. What's going on here?"

THE DOJO SPACE: BIRD'S-EYE VIEW

Organizations create dojos to help teams learn new practices and skills. They also invest in dojo spaces because they're trying to change the culture and the way information is shared. That happens more through networking and informal connections between people than it does through hierarchical organizational structures. Crosstalk is an effective catalyst for learning, and the dojo space encourages this type of informal exchange. For example, if you have five teams in a dojo at the same time, you don't want to completely isolate them from each other. The areas should be almost too close for comfort. You want team members to overhear conversations and jump in when they have something to contribute.

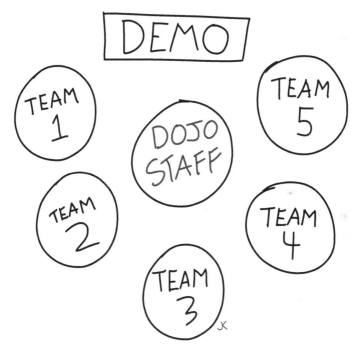

A sketch of what a floor plan might look like for a dojo, with multiple teams, a dojo staff area, and a demo area

Obviously, it can't be so noisy that no one can get any work done, but having an environment that allows for informal networks and connections to be made encourages serendipitous moments of light bulbs going off and ah-has. In one large dojo we coached in, classroom-sized whiteboards were placed between team areas to create walls. There were whiteboards on both sides so that teams could write on them. The teams could still overhear each other—to allow for those serendipitous moments—but not so much as to lose focus on their own activities.

When conversations are overheard, teams come to realize they're both trying to solve a similar problem, and they might start collaborating more. Try to create an environment that has the density for people to make these kinds of connections. There are those opportune moments where one team is heads down, working quietly and they overhear conversation from another team. If they have something to add to the conversation, they might chime in "Hey, we're trying to solve the same problem. Maybe we should collaborate on this."

There are three main areas to the dojo: the team space, the dojo staff space, and the demo space.

THE TEAM SPACE: ENCOURAGE SERENDIPITY

First and foremost, a dojo space is designed to stimulate and support learning and is well served by the same visual display tools that you find in a studio.

What a team space might look like in the dojo

Elements of the team space include:

- Whiteboards for having design discussions, sharing information, and creating new knowledge in the team
- Supplies to support both the work and the learning that's going to happen, such as sticky notes, butcher paper, markers, and dry-erase pens. Each team member needs to have their own laptop, which they usually bring themselves, so they can easily transition back out of the dojo and continue working. Laptops also aid in making the space more interactive and spontaneous—pairs and groups can dynamically form in different areas without being tethered to a desk.
- Places to hang information on the walls. Putting information in sight helps people learn and remember.

Much of the learning in the dojo includes externalized memory. Agile uses the term "information radiators"—we hang things on the wall that radiate information back into the team area.

- A large 4K television that has a dedicated computer or can easily connect to laptops, so whole teams can participate in group learning activities

The team space in a dojo differs from typical classroom settings and from standard workplace settings. Rather than sitting at single desks side-by-side, the team sits around one table and faces each other. Ideally, this would be a round table, not a long, rectangular table. You want to set up a dynamic where everyone feels like they have an equal seat at the table. At first, it can be disruptive to actually see the people you're working with—and that's good. Also, seeing who you're working with reinforces the idea that we're in this together. The dojo space encourages communication and teamwork over working alone.

There are no assigned seats in the team space. The space should be easy to reconfigure. The entire team may work on something together in the morning and then split into smaller groups in the afternoon. Those smaller groups should still be able to see each other and communicate together.

Many groups shy away from the idea of seeing each other

and communicating directly. We worked with one group where a developer was writing back-end code. He'd come talk to us rather than the front-end developer he was writing code for. The second time this happened, Joel suggested he try talking directly to the front-end developer. Another time, Dion remembers sitting between two people and hearing the pings of chat messages bouncing between them. When he realized they were chatting with each other electronically, he said, "Maybe get up and try talking to each other directly?"

Communication and disruption are encouraged in the dojo, and teams learn how to work and learn differently. Teams focus on outcomes for the group, not on individual tasks. We stress that everyone externalize their thinking and encourage using whiteboards and establishing common language.

WE DON'T HAVE THE SPACE YET

Setting up a dedicated dojo space is a big investment of time, money, and people. Some organizations, understandably, want to dip their toe into the dojo experience and see if it works before dedicating the resources to create a separate learning space. We've seen organizations use a large conference room for a trial dojo and, while it can be successful, it doesn't create the cross-team pollination that occurs in a dedicated space with multiple teams.

If you're unsure whether a dojo is right for your organization but are curious about the results a dojo experience could provide, we recommend running a trial before making the investment. We must emphasize the importance of making sure the trial has substance and creates an environment as close as possible to a true dojo. At least two teams should go through the dojo during overlapping six-week periods, and they should reside in a space that's large enough to hold both teams. By putting teams in a big conference room, the experience risks becoming little more than onsite training, and a dojo has far more benefits to offer.

SPACE FOR THE DOJO STAFF

In addition to space for the teams, a dojo has space for the dojo staff—the coaches, product manager, operations manager, and dojo manager—all of whom you'll read about in the next chapter.

The coaches spend most of their time with the teams, but they also need a space where they can sit when they're not working with teams or when they are learning something new themselves. The product manager, operations manager, and dojo manager all sit in the area with the coaches, allowing them all to work together on their product—the dojo. The dojo staff area has a similar setup to the team area.

MIT professor Thomas Allen developed a theory that looks at the effect of distance on communication between engineers. The Allen curve states that if you get more than sixty feet away from someone, you're less likely to get up and physically walk over and communicate with them. Ideally, if you have a very large space, this coaches' space would be located within sixty feet of the teams. While that sounds prescriptive and dogmatic, our experience validates the theory of the Allen curve.

We worked in one dojo that could hold twelve teams and was positioned in a long, narrow space. The coaches sat at one end of the space. Teams that were close to the coaches' space would walk over to talk to a coach if they had a question. Teams at the other end didn't do that; they would only approach the coaches if they happened to be walking by the coaches' space on their way to another destination. Placing the coaches' space in the middle of the team space would have been a better solution.

The dojo staff space is very similar to the space for teams learning in the dojo.

The dojo staff also need room to hang information on the walls, which might include reminders of outcomes for teams in the current dojo experience, the demo schedule, and a calendar showing teams' dojo schedules. The coaches meet here in the morning to discuss what they're doing with their teams and share information.

THE DEMO SPACE

In typical Agile-style development, teams do a demo or a review of what they've built at the end of a sprint. Even though we do two-and-a-half-day sprints, we still encourage teams to do brief fifteen- to twenty-minute demos at the end of every sprint.

The demo space is set off from the team space, but still near the same big open area, so teams can see when another team is doing a demo, get up and walk over, and attend the demo if they want to.

The demo space is large enough to encourage attendance from many people in the dojo.

The focal point of the demo space is a display area. Some dojos use a large screen and a projector. We've seen a dojo with a wall of nine monitors that acted as a single monitor. You want seating that allows everyone to see the display. It could be soft seating or chairs. We want this environment to be comfortable and feel cool and innovative, like a startup. People from outside the team, such as stakeholders, leaders, or business domain experts will often come to the demos because they're interested in seeing new products or a different technology. Depending on the size of the demo space and potential audience, you might want to include the option for a microphone.

We recommend posting a schedule of the week's demos. Teams in the dojo are often working on different but related products. People like to attend other teams' demos because they're interested in seeing new developments and what other teams are learning, particularly when they're working on something similar, from either a product or a learning perspective.

THE LOUNGE SPACE

The dojo promotes new ways of communicating and networking, and as team members get to know each other, they tend to seek places to hang out away from their team spaces.

You want to include an informal lounge area with soft seating where people can congregate. Some dojos place the lounge area near the kitchen, so people can grab something to drink and have conversations. The lounge is a place to make connections, share information with each other, or just relax and step out of the team space for a minute. Anyone in the dojo might use the lounge area to relax for a few minutes, including teams, coaches, the dojo manager, or the operations manager.

THE POWER OF INFORMAL GATHERING SPACES

In *The Psychology of Computer Programming*,[2] Gerald Weinberg tells a story about the effect of removing vending machines from an informal gathering space. (Jenny Quillien also quotes this story in *Clever Digs*.)

A university computing center had a large common space where students could work on programming problems. In the room next door, two graduate students provided help for difficult problems. Vending machines were set up at one end of the common space. At times, the noise level became quite loud and some people working in the common space began complaining about the noise.

The computing center manager went to the space to investigate the problem. He spent very little time there and returned to his office where he started working on having the vending machines removed. He also had signs installed instructing

2   Gerald Weinberg, *The Psychology of Computer Programming* (Weinberg & Weinberg, 2011).

students to be quiet in the common space.

The week after the machines had been removed, the manager received another complaint. Students were now complaining about the lack of help available for solving difficult problems. When the manager returned to the space, he saw lines coming out of the room where the graduate students sat, extending into the common space. When he spoke to the graduate students, they told him there were more people requesting help than there used to be.

Eventually, the manager figured out the root of the problem. It was the vending machines.

He discovered that when they had the vending machines, crowds of students would form around them. The students were having conversations about their programming problems and they were sharing information with each other. They were solving their problems among themselves. As a result, the load on the need for help from the graduate students was reduced to a level they could handle.

When the administrator removed the vending machines, he also removed the natural connections and information sharing that happens in these types of informal gathering spaces. The idea behind the soft-seating lounge space in a dojo is to intentionally create a space that fosters this kind of opportunity for collaborative learning.

The dojo space, floor plan, and seating arrangements encourage collaborative learning, but it is the dojo staff that guides teams through their dojo experience. The next chapter discusses the roles of the dojo staff, the responsibilities of each role, and the traits and skillset each role requires.

Chapter Five

DOJO ROLES

We like to think of our champions and idols as superheroes who were born different from us. We don't like to think of them as relatively ordinary people who made themselves extraordinary.

—CAROL S. DWECK, *MINDSET: THE NEW PSYCHOLOGY OF SUCCESS*

When an organization first creates a dojo, a few people can cover multiple roles. At a minimum, you'll want a dojo manager and coaches when you begin. When a dojo is in its early stages, a single person can pick the coaches, market the dojo, set the direction, and manage the team schedules. As the dojo grows from hosting one or two teams at a time to a permanent space with multiple simultaneous teams, one person doesn't have the bandwidth to manage the day-to-day operations and the long-range vision.

You may have people who can fill the various roles in your organization already, or you might have to hire outside consultants in the beginning to get your dojo up and running. At any time, a dojo may have a mix of internal and external people filling the roles. For example, you may choose to appoint internal employees in the dojo management roles and hire outside coaches at first, and then staff up as the dojo grows.

In the pages that follow, we take you through the roles one by one, describing the responsibilities and the type of person who best fits that role.

PRODUCT MANAGER

Everyone who works in a dojo should be thinking about the dojo as a product; however, the product manager has the primary responsibility for guiding the team to identify the offerings and practices teams will learn. A good product manager will shine if she focuses on creating offerings that help teams improve their ability to develop digital products.

The core responsibility of the product manager is to align the dojo offerings with the needs of the organization. The risk, especially in the early stages of a dojo, is that in an effort to fill the dojo with teams, the product manager becomes reactive and accepts any team, even when the dojo can't meet the team's needs. For example, the coaches might not have the skills to teach the practices the team wants to learn. Or teams are allowed to circumvent the intake process and come into the dojo without an understanding of the expectations.

As technology and product needs change, so should the offerings of the dojo. The product manager keeps an eye on technology developments so she can look ahead at the practices the dojo will need to support six to twelve months in the future. For example, many organizations are evaluating how to add artificial intelligence and machine learning to their products, but those are skills that few developers or product teams have. A forward-thinking product manager would look to add coaching around those skills to the dojo's suite of offerings now so the dojo is ready for an influx of teams interested in that technology.

The product manager acts as the main liaison with the rest of the organization for promoting the dojo and making sure the organization understands the dojo's products and services. The product manager will also help identify how the dojo's impact on the organization will be measured, and she will actively capture that information and communicate it to key stakeholders.

The person who fills the product manager role needs to have good communication and decision-making skills.

They need to understand the organization's business domain. They also need to understand enough about technology to be able to make effective decisions when defining offerings and practices the dojo will support.

COACHES

Knowledge is better created in the people who are trying to acquire it through face-to-face long-term mentoring kinds of relationships. If we really want the people who attend the dojo to develop an understanding of new concepts and be able to carry them forward after the dojo, they need the mentorship the dojo provides.

Coaches play the primary role in a dojo. Coaches guide the team through their learning journey, so teams can then learn on their own, rather than having coaches—or managers—tell them what to do. They teach the practices that need to be taught and help teams solve problems in their work while creating a path of learning.

By bringing their real-world work into the dojo, the team often uncovers constraints they didn't know existed. Coaches might be as surprised as the team is by the constraints in the environment or a problem with code. The coach helps the team respond to the situation in the moment, which leads to much deeper knowledge creation than a canned curriculum.

WHO MAKES A GOOD COACH?

Coaching, by its nature, requires soft skills such as active listening and the ability to ask engaging questions that lead to knowledge creation. Active listening involves being present and engaged in what the other person is saying rather than immediately jumping to conclusions and formulating a response. Active listening requires awareness and practice. Here lies the difference between coaches and trainers: dojo coaches meet the team where they are and respond to what happens in the moment, rather than teach a prescribed curriculum.

The ideal coach is a T-shaped person—having a breadth of skills—as opposed to an I-shaped person, who has depth in one or a few skills. Coaches with a breadth of skills across the entire product development value stream can help teams learn how practices are interrelated and support each other. They provide continuity for the team's learning because the team doesn't have to go to multiple coaches to learn different practices.

When coaches have only one skill, the organization must rotate different coaches through the team, which breaks continuity. For example, if you have one coach who understands how to build Java microservices, another coach who understands automating infrastructure setup, a third coach who understands testing, and maybe even a fourth coach who understands monitoring, you end up with either four coaches working with one team or a constant shuffling of coaches between different teams. When coaches shuffle from one team to another, they lose context of why certain decisions were made. When one broadly skilled coach works with a team, there is continuity in the coaching, which leads to better outcomes for the team's learning goals. Additionally, scheduling Tetris is unnecessary, as the one coach is there all the time.

That said, it is utopic in most organizations for one coach to function as the be-all and end-all coach for a team. As a result, most dojos are staffed with three different types of coaches with the following three skill domains, which correspond to the practices you want teams to learn:

- Product coaches coach teams on how to build the right products with good product/market fit. They work on product discovery skills and help teams learn how to validate product ideas along the entire product development value stream.
- Agile coaches (sometimes referred to as process coaches) coach teams on how to build a product from a process perspective. They help teams learn how to use the right process so they have quick feedback loops and can change direction quickly. Some Agile coaches have technical backgrounds and can help teams learn technical practices. Other Agile coaches don't have technical backgrounds and focus on help-

ing teams learn Agile and Lean processes. In general, they work in the delivery segment of the value stream.

· Technical coaches help teams build continuous delivery pipelines, write better quality code, and adopt specific technologies. They focus on engineering practices and, in general, help teams improve the practices and skills from the delivery segment through the deployment and operations segment of the value stream. (You may see some organizations with DevOps coaches. A DevOps coach is a technical coach who typically focuses on practices that start when code is committed and end when it is deployed and operating in a product environment.)

We advocate for coaches that have skills in two of the three domains. In our industry, the idea of coaching product discovery skills is relatively new. In today's environment, it's easier to find Agile and technical coaches, so we often teach Agile and technical coaches how to do product coaching.

If you have to hire three individual coaches for a single team, that's fine, but ideally you can hire one or two at the beginning. The goal is to have a coaching group that knows the practices and skills the teams coming into the dojo want to learn.

Dojo coaching takes a nuanced approach. While you may

find people on your existing staff who have experience with the practices and skills you want to offer in the dojo, not everyone has coaching skills. Team leads, architects, and engineers may be highly skilled in technical practices and great at their jobs, but that doesn't make them great coaches who can help others learn those practices. Even if your organization has people in roles you call "coaches," these people may focus only on helping teams learn and adhere to a process. Coaches need to resist a directive approach, and rather empower the team to be self-directed and responsible.

Companies that have adopted Agile, Scrum, SAFe, or some other methodology oftentimes have people in an Agile coaching role already. They reassign these people to the dojo as Agile coaches. Many coaches with an Agile background are delivery-focused; the company hired them because they believe the coaches can help them deliver faster. Switching to the dojo mindset can be challenging for Agile coaches because the dojo stresses learning over delivery. Coaching for learning is different than coaching for delivery. Success is defined as achieving learning goals, rather than meeting a release date or improving a team's velocity.

Finding coaches who can help teams learn not only process, but product and technical practices, is challenging. Most organizations don't have enough people with those skills. Initially, an organization may have to hire external coaches. As the dojo grows, the external coaches may become employees, or they may coach the employees and help them develop additional coaching skills.

THE COACH'S CAREER PATH

Conventional wisdom says that coaches have a vertical career progression. An Agile coach may work with a single team and then work on larger programs or platforms that require coordination between multiple teams. Over time, the coach moves up the organization, coaching entire business units and eventually reaching C-level coaching to help transform the entire organization.

We propose lateral development for a dojo coach, encouraging coaches with a deep technical knowledge to learn product discovery practices. Breadth makes dojo coaches far more effective working with teams because they can address more of the value stream. Likewise, coaches who are passionate product coaches are well served to enhance their skills with technical knowledge.

There's no reason why someone with a forty-year coaching career path ahead of them can't develop laterally across all of these skills rather than hierarchically moving up the org chart. Even a great Agile coach won't necessarily be good at working at the portfolio or C-level. Some coaches provide their best value at the team level. If a person provides value to your organization at that level, why would you encourage them to move into a role that they're not skilled for, nor really want to do?

HOW DO COACHES SPEND THEIR TIME?

At the beginning of the six weeks, the dojo experience is weighted toward product discovery practices to make sure teams are designing products well. In the second week, or sometimes at the end of the first week, process and technical practices come into play. In the first few weeks, coaches spend more hands-on time with the team, guiding their practices and processes and teaching specific practices. As the six-week period progresses, the team becomes more self-sufficient in learning by doing, and the coaches take on a more supportive role.

Time commitment from Agile and product coaches over the course of the six weeks looks like the following:

- High Touch: During a team's first two weeks in the dojo, we say the coaches are "high touch" with the team. This means that the coach spends the majority of their day with the team (six out of eight hours), either directly teaching and working with the team or just hanging out in the space with the team in case questions arise. It is important that the coach is with the team during these first weeks. New teams aren't comfortable coming to the coach, but when the coach is there consistently, the team will ask questions.

- Medium Touch: A team's second two weeks in the dojo are considered "medium touch." A coach spends roughly half their day with the team. The coach is teaching and guiding as needed, but the focus here is on seeing the teams start to embrace learning and exploring together and teaching each other.
- Low Touch: The final two weeks a team is in the dojo are considered "low touch." During this time, a coach spends more time observing and is available to answer questions. The focus for the coach during these two weeks is seeing the team own and apply their learnings and seeking new learnings together as they transition out of the dojo. A coach may be with a team just an hour or two per day in low touch.

High-, medium-, and low-touch coaching are ideals. While every team is different, the goal is the same—heavy teaching and guiding early on from the coach that tapers down as the team nears the end of the dojo, so the team is empowered to control their future.

Agile and product coaches will have a high, medium, low touch as mentioned above. Technical coaches, more often than not, have a "fat tail" with teams. Their first week will be medium touch, as there is more Agile and product learning happening. Once the team starts building their product, the technical coach shifts into high touch. This will last all of week two and into week three. More often than not, a technical coach will be medium touch with a team for the duration of the team's dojo experience.

	AGILE/PRODUCT COACH	TECH COACH
Week 1	High—80%	Medium—50%
Week 2	High—80%	High—80%
Week 3	Medium—50%	High—80%
Week 4	Medium—50%	Medium—50%
Week 5	Low—20%	Medium—50%
Week 6	Low—20%	Medium—40%

High-, medium-, and low-touch coaching for one team

Every dojo figures out its own unique cadence for how coaches work with teams and their level of engagement over the course of a six-week experience. Every organization finds its own balance for the number and types of coaches necessary to run the number of teams concurrently going through their dojo.

HOW MANY COACHES DO YOU NEED?

The number of coaches you need depends on the size of your dojo, the practices you want to teach, and the skills of your coaches. If you have one coach with broad skills, you could have one coach per team. Typically, each team has two coaches with overlapping skills: one technical coach and one Agile/product coach.

To start figuring out how many coaches you need and how many teams you can support concurrently, you will need to understand team size and coach time commitment. We expect coaches to be fully committed to the dojo and the team size to be between eight and twelve members. In the event the team is large (we had one team that had thirty members, for example) we use chartering and learning goals to create smaller teams while still adhering to all the desired attributes of a full-stack, cross-functional team.

Most dojos stagger the start of teams by a few weeks. You want your dojo to have density and a nice mix of teams in various weeks of their journey. We recommend most dojos start with staggering team starts by two weeks.

When a new team starts in your dojo, a product or Agile coach that is coaching another team in their fifth week could start with the new team. The original team the Agile coach was working with would keep their technical coach, and the new team would get a new technical coach.

	TEAM 1	TEAM 2
Week 1	Agile Coach 1–80% Tech Coach 1–50%	
Week 2	Agile Coach 1–80% Tech Coach 1–80%	
Week 3	Agile Coach 1–50% Tech Coach 1–80%	
Week 4	Agile Coach 1–50% Tech Coach 1–80%	
Week 5	Agile Coach 1–20% Tech Coach 1–50%	Agile Coach 1–80% Tech Coach 2–50%
Week 6	Agile Coach 1–20% Tech Coach 1–40%	Agile Coach 1–80% Tech Coach 2–80%
Week 7		Agile Coach 1–50% Tech Coach 2–80%
Week 8		Agile Coach 1–50% Tech Coach 2–80%
Week 9		Agile Coach 1–20% Tech Coach 2–50%
Week 10		Agile Coach 1–20% Tech Coach 2–40%

High-, medium-, and low-touch coaching for two teams with staggered start dates

The most common scheduling pattern in dojos is to have a new team start every two weeks. To achieve this level of density with two coaches per team, you then need a total of five coaches: two Agile/product coaches and three technical coaches.

	TEAM 1	TEAM 2	TEAM 3
Week 1	Agile Coach 1–80% Tech Coach 1–50%		
Week 2	Agile Coach 1–80% Tech Coach 1–80%		
Week 3	Agile Coach 1–50% Tech Coach 1–80%	Agile Coach 2–80% Tech Coach 2–50%	
Week 4	Agile Coach 1–50% Tech Coach 1–80%	Agile Coach 2–80% Tech Coach 2–80%	
Week 5	Agile Coach 1–20% Tech Coach 1–50%	Agile Coach 2–50% Tech Coach 2–80%	Agile Coach 1–80% Tech Coach 3–50%
Week 6	Agile Coach 1–20% Tech Coach 1–40%	Agile Coach 2–50% Tech Coach 2–80%	Agile Coach 1–80% Tech Coach 3–80%
Week 7		Agile Coach 2–20% Tech Coach 2–50%	Agile Coach 1–50% Tech Coach 3–80%
Week 8		Agile Coach 2–20% Tech Coach 2–40%	Agile Coach 1–50% Tech Coach 3–80%
Week 9			Agile Coach 1–20% Tech Coach 3–50%
Week 10			Agile Coach 1–20% Tech Coach 3–40%

High-, medium-, and low-touch coaching for multiple concurrent teams

When considering the number of coaches you'll need in your dojo, remember that the coaches need breaks. They can't work fifty-two weeks a year without a breather between teams. Not only do coaches burn out, but they also need the opportunity to learn new skills themselves. You want to build in a buffer so a coach gets a break every three to four teams. Technical coaches might need breaks more frequently to keep their skills current as the organization adopts new technology. This means you'll have a bench of coaches and, at any one time, some of them will not be working directly with teams. Using the earlier example with a team starting every two weeks, you may want to have seven coaches: three Agile/product coaches and four technical coaches. This would allow for that buffer to exist and support continual learning for the coaches.

COACHING THE COACH

Dojos are a big investment for companies, so they're intended to be around for years, not months. When a dojo is new, the external consultants who coach the teams can help develop your internal coaching staff. When we help clients set up their dojo, we coach their coaches. At a certain point in time, you'll probably have really good coaches, and it makes sense to use your dojo to develop additional coaching capability.

We onboard new coaches following an "observe, pair, lead" progression toward competency.

In an ideal world, a new coach may be ready to coach a team on their own after pairing with an experienced coach working with three teams. In our experience, it is much more fluid than that. Before a new coach starts with a team, experienced coaches walk the new coach through how the dojo works, what practices are taught, and why those practices were chosen. The new coach will then be paired with an experienced coach starting with a team. The new coach observes the experienced coach lead the team through chartering and early activities. The experienced coach works with the team, but also takes breaks and talks to the junior coach to explain what he's doing and how he's guiding the team. He explains his thought process, what he sees happening with the team, and why he's decided to coach the team in certain ways. This gives the new coach the opportunity to ask questions. That new coach may lead some of the day-to-day learning for the first team they pair on, but the new coach would not be on their own.

Knowledge exchange between experienced coaches and junior coaches has to happen in the moment. It's tacit knowledge exchange, requiring feedback, reflection, and validation that the guidance is getting through.

When the next team starts, the new coach will pair with the more experienced coach on the consult and the charter. The new coach will lead some parts of these practices, with the experienced coach there to assist. Experienced coaches have to see how junior coaches interact with, react to, and guide a team when new things come up, in order to provide helpful feedback. The experienced coach will lead other parts of the practices and discuss with the new coach why they asked certain questions and how they led the team's experience.

This pairing of experienced coaches with junior coaches goes on for a few teams until the new coach has led all of the consults and chartering, and guided the day-to-day learning for a team and feels comfortable on their own.

It may take four or five teams, depending on the coach and their comfort level, but there is a natural progression seen in immersive learning environments: observe the practice, pair with another coach on the practice, and then lead the practice.

Observation and feedback on how people are coaching should continue even with experienced coaches. No matter their level of experience, we encourage coaches to observe each other to get a different perspective and ask why someone took one approach over another. Sometimes you learn new tactics to add to your bag of tricks; other times you validate an approach that works for you.

The process is never-ending. The dojo is about continuous learning; it would be hypocritical for coaches to ignore this mindset for their own work.

OPERATIONS MANAGER

The operations manager is responsible for running the day-to-day aspects of the dojo. Organizations are often tempted to skimp on this role because of its administrative nature, but without the operations manager, the dojo can come to a standstill. Someone who already works in your organization can likely take on this role. We've seen some companies assign skilled executive administrators or coordinators to this role.

The operations manager monitors how well the physical space is working. She works to make sure the space is comfortable and is working for the teams and the coaches. She ensures the dojo is stocked with supplies, including printer paper, markers, whiteboards, notepads, and the right furniture. As the dojo grows—say more teams are coming in or new types of work are being done, like robotics—she works on changing the space to meet these evolving needs.

In some dojos, the operations manager has taken over the "personality" of the dojo, creating special events like afternoon stretches or cookie breaks. This all adds to the character of the dojo as a fun place to be.

In most places, the operations manager is also involved in scheduling teams for initial consultations, chartering, and their dojo experience. This person deals with the challenges of making sure the space is available, that the right coaches are assigned to teams, and that teams aren't waiting months to begin.

The operations manager may meet with teams during overviews and consultations to explain the initial concept of the dojo, how it works, and what the next steps are. Responsibilities may include marketing and brand awareness for the dojo. In many organizations, this person is also the first and biggest dojo evangelist.

It's important that the person has experience handling logistics, is organized, and is detail-oriented. The operations manager will interact with the dojo staff, the organization's leaders, and the teams coming into the dojo, so they need to be a people person. Lastly, they are good listeners and observers—seeing what teams and coaches need in the dojo and providing things, in many cases before those groups even know they need them.

DOJO MANAGER

The dojo manager is responsible for staffing and developing coaches. She works with the product manager to ensure the dojo is staffed with enough coaches to meet the demand of the teams who want to come into the dojo. She also ensures she's hiring a staff with all the skills necessary to support all the practices the dojo teaches. She looks out for the health of the coaches to make sure no one is getting burned out. She also ensures coaches have their own learning plans and are getting time to accomplish their learning goals.

Most dojos have between three and eight teams in a physical space in a single location. Some organizations create multiple dojos so that various locations will have a dojo and each dojo will have multiple teams. When dojos reach that scale, the role of a dojo manager becomes vital.

The need for synchronization and sharing offerings and experiences across dojos, as well as staffing needs and projections, grows as the number of teams and locations supported grows. In a large organization with multiple locations, the dojo manager instills mechanisms for communication to happen across all the dojos. For example, if coaches see a problem in one location, they can communicate with coaches in another location to see if teams in other locations experience the same problem. The problem can then be resolved across all dojos.

Obviously, this person needs to understand what the dojo is as a product and service—she needs to understand everything in this book—and have strong management skills. Ideally, she's got a mix of knowledge about technology and product as well.

Additionally, the dojo manager is someone who's interested in transforming the company. She wants to see the organization improve, the culture change, and the engineering and product management skills improve. She's a transformation leader, not someone who follows the status quo.

The dojo manager has to be comfortable with the dojo's dynamic nature and knowing that she won't always have the answers, nor will technology and business objectives stay consistent over time. She has to be comfortable with the idea that there is no standard curriculum in the dojo, and that it's a different type of learning environment. Someone heavily invested in traditional training would *not* be a good fit.

To recap, a dojo offers coaching around practices that enable teams to develop skills. The product manager, operations manager, and dojo manager facilitate the development and administration of the dojo, while the coaches spend the most amount of time with the teams. Initially, the dojo offering may include one set of practices the coaches are skilled in teaching. Over time, the dojo will evolve, and the number of practices and offerings will expand as more coaches come on board, more teams come into the dojo, and product and technology needs change. In the next chapter, you'll learn how to generate interest in your dojo and how the dojo staff vets teams that are interested in coming into the dojo.

Chapter Six

INTAKE: GETTING TEAMS READY

Unless commitment is made, there are only promises and hopes...but no plans.

—PETER DRUCKER, *MANAGEMENT*

We were called in to help an organization with their dojo. Three teams had already gone through the dojo experience and, while those experiences had gone well, the results were not as stellar as the organization thought they would be. The early teams had automated some infrastructure setup, with the thought that many other teams would be able to reuse their work. What the organization learned, though, was that other teams were not reusing the work.

We observed the first day of another team's dojo experience. We asked them why they were in the dojo. The team said they wanted to learn how to improve automation of infrastructure deployment and configuration—more specifically, automating the creation of a new virtual machine and deploying the Tomcat application server to it. Fair enough, but we wanted a more outcome-focused answer. We adjusted the question and asked why they were learning infrastructure automation. They didn't have an answer and continued to say they wanted to learn how to automate infrastructure deployment and configuration.

We tried again. We explained the practices and skills they learn in the dojo need to have a purpose and a context that links to an outcome they are trying to achieve. No one could reference any desired outcomes or impact they wanted to have for their team or for the organization. The closest thing we got to an answer was that the company was adopting DevOps, so the teams felt like they should learn infrastructure automation.

We asked the previous teams the same question and discovered they all had the same answer. Their intention was to learn a skill—and they'd learned a skill—but they had no sense of why they had learned it. When we explored why other teams weren't using the infrastructure automation that was created, they said, "It's too complicated, it breaks too often, and it doesn't work the way we'd like it to work."

Why were teams spending six weeks in the dojo, learning new skills and building things no one would use? The teams thought it was enough to learn new skills. It's great to learn new skills, but without defining the outcomes you're trying to achieve, you're learning for learning's sake. With these teams, people were learning how to automate infrastructure setup, but the learnings weren't having an impact on the organization.

In the early days of this dojo, teams that expressed interest in participating in a dojo experience just started one day. They didn't go through an intake process that creates a common understanding of what they want to learn, why they want to learn it, and what outcome they expect to achieve by learning it.

Before teams enter a dojo, we want them to define their learning goals and expected outcomes for their dojo experience. We want to understand why they want to learn specific practices and skills. We want to ensure learning those practices and skills is tied to intended outcomes for the team and for the organization. Without that context, teams go through a dojo experience as if it were traditional training. Success is defined as completing the training, and the possibility for having impact is lost, or accidental at best.

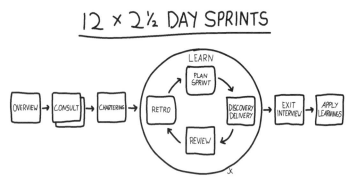

How a team flows through a dojo

A successful dojo experience begins before the team even knows what a dojo is. Educating teams on the theory and structure behind a dojo experience is the first step to helping them reach their desired goals. When a team understands what a dojo is before starting their experience, they have realistic expectations about their required commitment and what the dojo offers.

We call the first phase of the dojo experience the *intake process*, which takes teams from awareness of the dojo through exploratory conversations to specific goal-setting conversations. We'll talk about the overview and consult stages in this chapter and then present chartering, which is a more involved stage, in chapter 7.

THE INTAKE PROCESS IN ACTION

Intake comprises three parts: creating awareness, which occurs during the overview; setting expectations and learning about the team, which happen during the consult; and creating alignment, which takes place during chartering.

Here's how the intake process could go for a team.

An engineering manager with eight teams learns about the dojo from an internal podcast about company news. She comes and talks to the dojo staff (the operations manager and a coach) for a half hour. They talk about her teams, the improvements she thinks need to be made, and why she might be interested in having one of her teams come into the dojo. The dojo staff ask questions to determine whether her teams would be a good fit for the dojo. They explain the dojo is about learning more than delivery and ask if she has any teams that need to learn new practices and improve their skills. The engineering manager says she has a team that's scheduled to start a new development effort in a month that doesn't have a critical deadline and that the team is interested in learning automated testing practices and improving their continuous delivery pipeline. The dojo staff tell her this team is a good candidate for the dojo.

The dojo operations manager schedules a consult with

the whole team a week after meeting with the engineering manager. The coach meets with the team for an hour and explains the dojo concept. He also asks what they're interested in learning and discusses the development effort that they'll begin in a few weeks. Expectations are set that they will come into the dojo to work on their new development effort.

The coach does a quick inventory of who does what on the team and asks if the team depends on anyone outside of the group to accomplish their tasks. In this case, the team has all the skills they need to deliver their product, so there's no need to talk about making additional people part of their dojo experience. If everything goes smoothly in the consult and the team wants to move forward with going through a dojo experience, we schedule the next step in the intake process, the four-hour chartering activity (covered in the next chapter).

OVERVIEW: BUILDING AWARENESS

The activities that take place during the overview phase of the intake process are designed to explain the dojo in an informal way to generate deeper interest from product development teams. They include reaching out to new audiences as well as speaking to established contacts who've already expressed an interest in your dojo. We call this phase the "overview" because it's exactly that. At this point, we're giving someone an overview of what the dojo is and how it works. Sometimes this is one person, sometimes it's a group of people, and sometimes it's a few team members from the same team.

Much as we like to believe people will beat down the door as soon as we build something new, the truth is you have to let potential customers know your product or service is available in order to generate interest that leads to an eventual purchase. In other words, you have to market your dojo to your internal product development teams to build awareness and interest.

Marketing is the job of the entire dojo staff. It's not as hard as it sounds, although it's often a challenge for the dojo staff to do marketing because it's not something they've done in the past. Partnering with the marketing staff within an organization can be a helpful way for the dojo staff to learn about marketing, especially in the early stages of a dojo.

Here are some ways the dojo staff can market the dojo to their internal customers:

- Speak about the dojo at internal conferences or town halls within your organization.
- Release an email campaign to stakeholders, team leaders, and/or developers.

- Create and hang posters in the departments where your potential customers work or hang out.
- Host a lunch for a general audience to announce the dojo is coming and give a presentation to explain what the dojo is.
- Meet with executives and managers to explain how the dojo can help their teams.
- Meet with engineers to explain the skills they could learn in the dojo.
- Host open houses in your dojo space.
- Host or participate in an internal blog or podcast.

You're limited only by your creativity, and these are just a few ideas to get you started.

Like any marketing campaign, you want to generate excitement and interest, and you do that by creating a message that speaks to the needs of your organization's product development teams. For example, if your teams are struggling with testing and deployments, mention how the dojo will work with teams to help them learn how to create suites of automated tests and automate their deployments. If you want people to come to your dojo, you have to make sure they understand the value the dojo can provide for them. They also need to hear how the dojo is different than traditional training and a little bit about how it works.

Marketing doesn't end just because someone has expressed interest in the dojo. You may have to follow up with someone several times after the initial overview to encourage them to bring their team into the dojo. When someone asks for more information or, better yet, comes in for a consult, you have to continue to sell them on the idea that the dojo experience is a good thing for them to buy (even if there's no direct cost to them).

WORD-OF-MOUTH MARKETING

The teams who go through the dojo experience can be your best marketing tool. A team that has a good dojo experience and feels supported afterward will talk about and promote their experience to other teams in your organization. The best advertising is still word of mouth. If a team that's gone through the dojo experience sees fellow teams struggling, they'll suggest that a dojo experience might help them. The ripple effect of teams talking about their success and suggesting the dojo is powerful.

Negative impressions often spread even faster than positive ones. Do everything you can to provide your teams with a positive experience. Make sure your dojo is staffed well. If you have early success with the teams who come to your dojo, it's tempting to scale quickly. If, however, you hire coaches who aren't experienced or haven't had time to work with senior coaches and learn how to run dojo experiences, your teams won't have the best six-week experience they could. Negative word of mouth can harm your dojo as much as positive word of mouth can help it.

GETTING BUY-IN FROM LEADERSHIP

You may find that teams are interested and excited about what the dojo experience can do for them, but leadership is hesitant to support their teams spending time in the dojo. In most cases, it's because they are afraid there will be a significant loss in output from the team over the six weeks they are in the dojo. Dojo staff can use this fear to start conversations around the value that will come from the team's learning in the dojo, and how that learning will increase quality, reduce cycle times, and potentially even increase output in the long run. It's important to be sympathetic to people in leadership roles when they are hesitant. They may have performance goals they are expected to achieve.

The dojo staff can provide content for the directors and executives who lead teams by taking them through half-day mini-dojo offerings with hands-on, experience-based learning. By going through these offerings, they can get a feel for what their teams will be or are experiencing—both before the dojo and while teams are in the dojo. Set up safe and easy exercises, so executives understand the problems the dojo is trying to solve. Explain why you're teaching teams the practices they're learning.

For example, we had a group of executives that came into a four-hour workshop and went through exercises where they learned how to automate patching a Linux box. We explained that we were going to patch a security vulnerability. The executives had heard about these things, and when we asked them how long it usually takes to patch their servers, they would say, "It feels like it takes years. It feels like we're always patching. We never stop patching servers because it takes so long and it's so painful."

They didn't understand the nuances of the work, nor did they need to, but they understood the pain involved and that patching was taking up a lot of capacity. We walked them through what we teach their teams and explained why we were teaching their teams infrastructure automation.

We showed these leaders how to write a two-line command to apply a patch to an existing server. We then gave them an unpatched system and told them they had to patch it. We said, "What would you normally do?" They laughed and explained what normally happens. The risk team gets involved and they send out alerts and emails. A ticket gets opened and people have to start tracking time against it, and so on. We explained that they should type two lines, as their teams would do, to apply and automate the patch. They did and saw the change that happens: their servers are patched. They said, "Wow, that was way simpler than I thought it had to be."

Your executives don't have to know about the technologies at play. They begin to understand what you're teaching the teams and why it's important. You expose them to practices the teams are learning and they begin to understand why it's worth investing in their teams' learning.

CONSULTS: SETTING EXPECTATIONS AND LEARNING ABOUT THE TEAM

When a team or team leader responds to your efforts to drive awareness of what the dojo is and they express interest in learning how the dojo could help their teams, it's time to schedule a consult to move the team toward a dojo experience.

Assuming you think a team is a good fit, you'll be selling them on the idea of coming into the dojo. If the initial conversation happens with a curious team member, you might need a follow-up meeting with their leadership before the full consult. You want to make sure there is enough support from leadership to move forward with a consult.

During the overview, you've likely spoken to the team manager or one person on the team. During the consult, the entire team needs to participate. You'll explain what a dojo is and explore ways in which the dojo can help the team improve their product delivery. The dojo is about learning in the context of real product delivery, so you'll explore what the team could work on while learning new practices. You'll want to ensure the team is not up against a tight delivery deadline that would not allow time for learning. You'll also have a high-level conversation about what the team is interested in learning and improving, to make sure their interests align with your dojo offerings.

In addition, you want to make sure they understand how the dojo works and what kind of commitment they're signing up for. You want them to understand that the dojo is about learning over delivery and explain what their experience will be like from week to week and on a daily basis.

It is always great to provide examples that teams can relate to. Once you have had a few teams through your dojo, use them to help new teams understand what the dojo experience could be like for them. Tell stories about what teams have accomplished in the dojo—what products they delivered, what they learned, what improvements they made, and even what was challenging for them and how they worked through those challenges.

Ideally, during the consult you'll learn that the team would be a good fit for a dojo experience and the team will decide to commit to going through a dojo experience. Assuming they do, the operations manager will start working with the team to schedule chartering and the start of their six-week experience.

Teams might not be ready to commit to a dojo experience after going through a consult. They may decide their delivery deadlines are too tight to allow for learning, or they might realize the product they're working on has strong dependencies on people outside their team. There might be follow-up work to see if some of the people they are dependent on could be part of their dojo experience. Or they might simply want to think about it before committing.

In some cases, it may be necessary to have several consults with the team before they are ready to commit. Keep in touch with them and do what you can to help remove roadblocks that prevent them from coming into the dojo. Sometimes, several months may go by before a team is ready to commit.

DO THIS

The consult lasts about an hour. You'll explain how the dojo works and answer their questions. You'll also ask your own questions, which include, but aren't limited to, the following:

- How did you learn about the dojo?
- What products are you working on?
- How does work flow into and through the team? When and where are you engaged?
- What do you hope to learn in the dojo?
- What's preventing you from learning in your day-to-day work?
- What is your desired goal or outcome? How will what you learn in the dojo impact your team and the organization?
- Are you willing and able to commit to spending six to eight hours a day for six weeks in the dojo?

FAQ: GENERAL INTAKE QUESTIONS

Many teams ask similar questions when inquiring about a dojo, and the questions could come up at any time during the intake process—in the overview phase at an event or when someone stops by, as well as in the consult or chartering phases. We've given you some tips below for answering common questions.

- Why do teams have to be in the dojo the whole day?
  - A full day creates focused time where the team is learning and working together. The dojo loses its effectiveness when teams spend fewer than six hours in the immersive learning environment. In addition, a dojo is about team learning. We don't want teams thinking

some of them can attend in the morning, while others could attend in the afternoon.

- What about our other work?
  - You bring all of your work into the dojo. The dojo helps teams incorporate continuous learning into the way they work. If the team needs dedicated time for support or other responsibilities, we'll work that into the daily schedule.
- The team has a deadline in a month. How can they work around that?
  - The best solution is to schedule the dojo experience after the deadline has been met. External time constraints or preset commitments will affect the team's ability to learn and explore.
- Why six weeks?
  - Learning and retention happen with repetition. We've found through experimentation that six weeks is long enough for new practices to stick and to make significant improvements in the way teams work.
- Does everyone on the team have to be there the whole time?
  - Yes, everyone needs to be there the whole time. The dojo is about building shared understanding, having multiple perspectives from people with different skills involved every step of the way, and moving the whole team toward product ownership.
- Who pays for the dojo?
  - Most of the organizations we've been in fund the dojo

out of a general learning and development budget and don't charge teams on an individual basis to participate in the dojo. Your organization may be different; be ready to answer this question.

CHOOSING TEAMS FOR THE DOJO EXPERIENCE

Obviously, you want teams that are interested in the dojo to participate. Ideally, teams entering the dojo have specific outcomes that learning skills in the dojo could help them achieve.

Consider the following when choosing teams:

- Is the team open to learning and experimenting with new ways of working?
- Is the team free from deadlines that would make having time for learning difficult?
- Is the team working on something that could be used as an example for other teams to learn from?
- Will the team be able to be co-located in the dojo together?
- Is the team made up of mostly employees? (If the team is made up primarily of contractors, do you want to invest in helping the contractors improve their skills? We can't answer this for you. If you view them as long-term partners, you might want to have them go through the dojo. If they are short-term contrac-

tors, you probably don't want to make that investment in their learning.)

- Does this team provide products or services used by other teams in the organization? Will helping the team learn to create better products have a multiplier effect on the rest of the organization?
- Would this team be good evangelists for the dojo?

SELECTING YOUR FIRST TEAM

Few people want to be the first to do something, and it's no different for a dojo. When your organization decides to start a dojo, no matter how much great marketing you do, you may find you have a hard time getting the first team to go through the experience. As you talk to teams throughout your organization, keep an eye out for one that would be a good first-team candidate. You may have a team that is eager for transformation. They may not explicitly say they want the dojo experience, but they are open to conversations about improving their product development practices.

You want to choose a pilot team that is neither too easy nor too hard. If the team's goals are too easy, you risk being seen as successful only because the goals were easy. If they're too hard, you risk setting up the team and yourself for frustration, failure, and dissatisfaction. You want a team that has a problem of substance, that's interested in learning some of the practices you teach, and that will be able to demonstrate value from going through the dojo.

You'll also benefit by selecting a team aligned with organizational initiatives. For example, if your organization is just starting to migrate applications to the cloud, try to get a team doing a cloud migration to do it in the dojo. (Assuming, of course, you have coaches who can help the teams learn how to do cloud migrations.) It's likely you'll run into dependencies with other teams and may even experience some friction with governance and security groups. If you help the team work through these constraints and learn how to use the cloud platform, you'll be well on your way to creating demand for your dojo offerings.

The next chapter walks you through helping the team get aligned around what they want to learn and how the dojo will help them make progress toward their desired outcomes.

Chapter Seven

CREATING ALIGNMENT: CHARTERING

We have to grasp not only the Know-How but also "Know Why", if we want to master the Toyota Production System.

—SHIGEO SHINGO, *A STUDY OF THE TOYOTA PRODUCTION SYSTEM*

After the team has gone through the consult and is committed to a dojo experience, we schedule a chartering session with the team.

The main purpose of chartering is to make sure there is shared understanding of what a successful dojo experience looks like for the team. It's important that the dojo staff, team members, and the team's leadership and stakeholders all agree on what success is before the dojo experience starts. During chartering, we agree on what the team will deliver, what they will learn, and how they will work for the six weeks they'll spend in the dojo. This sets the team up for success before they even begin.

Chartering happens a week before the team starts their dojo experience. During chartering, dependencies may be discovered that need to be addressed before the team starts. The dependency could be as simple as getting everyone access to environments, code repositories, or tools. It could also involve negotiating time for other teams to work on dependent tasks related to the dojo team's product development.

In our experience, it's best not to charter more than two weeks prior to the start of a dojo experience. The longer the gap is between chartering and when the team starts, the higher the risk of significant changes that will impact the team. Outcomes a team previously aligned around might no longer be relevant and you may have to charter a second time.

Part of guiding a team through chartering is finding a balance between assessing what the team already knows, empowering them to define their own learning goals, and making suggestions about practices and skills they could learn that might not even be on their radar.

How much guidance a team needs around defining their

learning goals will vary from team to team. Some teams have a clear idea of the practices they want to learn. For example, during chartering, they say something like "We want to learn microservices, infrastructure automation, and test-driven design." Other teams aren't as clear about the specific practices they want to learn. They might say, "This is our current situation. We are trying to get our product deployed in the cloud with a new feature. We're not sure exactly where or what kind of help we need. We do know that things could be better, and we're looking for help from the dojo on how we could produce better outcomes or exit the death spiral of continuous testing."

Chartering lasts about four hours, divided into four fifty-minute working sessions and ten-minute breaks. The team must be engaged during the fifty minutes, which means laptops and phones closed; they can check their email and social media during the ten-minute breaks. A dojo coach leads the team through the different parts of chartering that define the learning experience that will happen in the dojo, how the team will work together, and what success looks like. The chartering agenda includes these specific items:

CHARTERING AGENDA

Team Name	Architecture Diagram and Tech Stack
Timeframe	Skills Matrix
Elevator Pitch	Logistics
Goals and Measures	Working Agreements
Community Map	

TEAM NAME

The first part of chartering is coming up with a team name. This is an icebreaker, a way to set the tone, indicating that it's okay to have fun in the dojo, and a way to define the team's identity in the dojo as being unique and different from their day-to-day work. It's also an opportunity for the coach to see how the team interacts. Often, the team's first attempt is an acronym for their system (e.g., POS Team for a point of sale system). Encourage them to come up with a name that reflects what they're working on or a metaphor for the work they're learning. They should choose a creative name they can rally around. We've had teams named Team Atom or Cloudtallica, for example.

The ease with which the team comes up with a name provides a subtle indicator of how clear they are about their purpose and how well they work together. If they have difficulty coming up with a name, they may have difficulty aligning around outcomes and learning goals. If different team members use different names or different metaphors, that may indicate a lack of team alignment. The name should also be appropriate for the work they're doing. If the team is doing work on a mainframe, it wouldn't make much sense if they called themselves Cloudtallica. The name unifies the team and gives them an identity in the dojo. Some dojos have gone so far as to print laptop stickers or even make T-shirts for teams with their team names on them.

TIMEFRAME

The timeframe has two parts: the start and end dates of the dojo experience, and the timeframe for product delivery, which often extends beyond the dojo. For example, the team may be working on a product with a three-month delivery timeframe that begins in the dojo, but it's clear to everyone on the team and all stakeholders that delivery will continue after the dojo experience has ended.

COACHING TIP

Write the start and end dates on the whiteboard, so the team can see it throughout chartering. Seeing the specific dates makes people think consciously about what can be accomplished within those dates. They may remember other events that are scheduled to occur within those dates that will impact their capacity for learning and product delivery. Visually seeing the dates also helps the team be more realistic about learning goals.

We want to reinforce the idea of the time commitment established during the consult to make sure no one's gone for two weeks during the six-week period. You also document any previous commitments or planned absences, such as one person who will be gone for a scheduled vacation. If you find many people will be absent during the six weeks, it may be a good idea to reschedule the dojo experience to a time when the whole team can be present.

ELEVATOR PITCH

The elevator pitch can be the hardest—and most important—part of chartering. Here, the team expresses the purpose of their time together in the dojo. The elevator pitch conveys what they're doing and, more importantly, why they're doing it. Most teams can quickly answer the *what* but have difficulty with the *why*.

The dojo coach starts by explaining the purpose of the pitch to the team, saying, for example, "We are looking to make sure we all understand why we are working together in the dojo for six weeks." To further help the team start thinking this through, the coach asks the team, "Imagine you just stepped into an elevator with your CEO and she asked what you were working on and why. What would you tell her? Why would that be interesting to her?"

There are four elements every elevator pitch contains:

- What the team is delivering
- Who they're delivering it for
- Why they're delivering that capability or feature
- What they are going to learn while delivering it

Here's an example for a hotel booking application:

> We're going to give our reward members the ability to pay for rooms with a combination of points and cash. We're adding this capability because our reward members have requested it and to keep parity with other reward programs. While we are delivering this capability, we're learning test-driven development and functional test automation to reduce product outages caused by defects.

To get to a cohesive elevator pitch, the coach will need to guide the team by asking probing questions. Usually, it's easy for the teams to define what they are delivering. Often, however, they have no idea why they are delivering that capability. It may be necessary to simply ask the team, "Why are you delivering this now?" In addition, you may have to ask, "Who do you expect to use this feature or capability?" to get them to define who they're delivering the capability for.

Initially, the coach is simply capturing the ideas the team is expressing. This can be done verbally, or you can use other techniques, such as having everyone write their ideas on sticky notes in silence for five minutes and then start combining the ideas as a group. In a sense, crafting the elevator pitch starts as a group brainstorming session. Once the team has expressed all their ideas, the ideas can be discussed and turned into a pitch.

Guiding teams to craft their elevator pitch takes time and strong coaching skills. It also takes practice. Understanding the mechanics of creating an elevator pitch is easy. Helping teams craft elevator pitches fostering shared understanding and creating alignment is not as easy as it might appear.

When teams are struggling, we sometimes use fill-in-the-blank exercises. If a team is struggling to define its high-level learning goals, we might use this format:

Currently _____ (pain) is happening, caused by _____ (problem). We believe by learning _____ (skill or practice), _____ (outcome) will happen.

If the team agrees on the challenge, they can craft a hypothesis that by learning something and then applying that learning, they'll have a better outcome. These statements help teams focus on the essence of the problem, not just the feature they want to build or the skill they want to learn.

In chartering, we begin to introduce the idea of the product development value stream and how the product is intended to lead to outcomes from both a business perspective and a customer-value perspective. Everyone on the team should be able to answer questions that explain the four elements of the elevator pitch and why the team is in the dojo.

This anecdote illustrates what can happen when there is a lack of alignment:

> Years ago, we were working on a long, traditional, waterfall development effort. We were about three years into it, and an ongoing argument began between one of the testers and one of the developers. The tester opened a defect in the defect-tracking tool. The developer rejected it and said, "It's not a defect. It's coded to spec." The tester would reopen the defect, and the developer would reject it. This happened several times and, finally, one of them said, "We can't just keep rejecting and reopening this defect." They turned to one of the business experts involved, and the three of them sat down to resolve the issue.
>
> Tester: "Look. This isn't working right."
>
> Developer: "It's coded to spec."
>
> Business expert: "This is what we're trying to do."
>
> Developer: "Well, if I had known that's what you were trying to accomplish with this requirement, I could have done it this other way. It would have been easier to develop, it would be better for the users, and we wouldn't have had this confusion."

It would have been better had that conversation happened before people invested time, money, and effort into the product. People need to understand the desired outcomes and the intended benefit—*why* they're doing something—before any of the work begins. The elevator pitch synthesizes both the *what* and the *why* of their time in the dojo.

When teams get this, it's a game changer.

Once teams have this shared understanding of where they are going and why, they can quickly rally around solving real problems together. The separation of roles goes out the window, and the focus shifts away from delivering "according to spec" to achieving valuable outcomes. This alignment drives great learning experiences and it helps teams create great products.

Remember: during chartering, the group takes breaks every fifty minutes. Your first break might happen while creating the elevator pitch, which gives the team a few minutes to reflect on their thoughts. Find a good point to pause, but don't feel like the team has to complete the pitch before they take their first break.

GOALS AND MEASURES

Goals and measures support the elevator pitch. Goals are defined for both the product and for the team's desired learning outcomes. The measures give us a way for determining if we've hit the goal or not. The elevator pitch helps us create alignment and shared understanding of what we're trying to accomplish at a high level. Goals and measures are more specific and, like the elevator pitch, they help us create a common understanding of what success looks like.

Here's an example: a team might already have a continuous delivery pipeline before they enter the dojo. However, it might take a long time to complete because there are manual steps. Their goal might be stated as "Reduce the time it takes the pipeline to run." The measure might be "Reduce the cycle time from code commit to the code being deployed by 20 percent."

To help teams get started, we'll ask them to imagine it's the end of their dojo experience and they're super happy with everything that happened. What stories will they tell someone about the things they did inside the dojo? What examples will they give? The questions framed as looking back on their experience from the future guide the team to think about goals and measures.

The team may come up with a narrative about what they want to achieve. For example, "The dojo was great. We were able to get a better understanding of our product and how to make it easier for our customers. We have fewer defects and we're able to deploy our product automatically." We ask them to go further and explain how they made the product easier to use for their customers. They might say, "We all understand our product better and why problems with some parts of the workflow were causing so many calls into our call center. By understanding the customer and the workflow better, we have been able to reduce the volume of calls. We were able to write some automated tests around this experience and are able to deploy our own code whenever we want to."

Imagining a story like that leads to ideas for goals. In the above example, we could have goals for understanding the customer better, writing automated tests, and automating deployments. Of course, each goal would have one or more measures that allow us to assess whether the goal was met. Let's say the team says, "We want to learn how to do test automation." That's fine as a goal, but how will they know they've learned test automation? The measure may be as simple as "We have X number of automated tests" or "We've automated 40 percent of the tests we run as part of our manual test suite." It would be even better if the team could tie the goal back to a measure with impact (see chapter 3). For example, the team might be tracking the change failure rate and tie improvements back to automated testing: "We want to reduce the change failure rate by 30 percent."

Frequently, teams will come up with measures they want to track, but they haven't established a baseline yet. That is fine. One of the reasons we charter a week before a team starts is for these types of situations. If a team does not have a baseline, they might be able to create one during the week before the dojo starts.

Each goal needs to have at least one measure, but frequently will have more than one. A team in the dojo should have a few goals: around three product-related goals and three learning goals, for a total of six goals, is a good start. If the team is struggling with their goals, a coach can make suggestions to get them started. However, you want the team to own their own learning, so you don't want the coach defining all the goals and measures.

COMMUNITY MAP

We view product communities as consisting of three primary perspectives, which we borrow from design thinking: viability, desirability, and feasibility. To ensure we have adequate representation for all three perspectives, we work with the team to create a community map.

Visually, the community map is a Venn diagram where each circle represents a different perspective of the product the team is working on:

- The viability circle represents the investors or the people who understand the business value of the product. For example, this group of people is able to provide perspective on the financial implications of delaying the release of features, or how much "too much" is, from a cost perspective.
- The desirability circle represents people who understand the customer and the value the customer derives from the product. People in this group understand how to learn what the customer wants from the product and how the product stacks up against the competition.
- The feasibility circle represents the group of people who understand the technical implications for delivering the product. They understand options for how the product can be delivered and can identify whether or not current systems and components will need to change in order to deliver the product.

We draw a Venn diagram on the board and label the circles.

We then ask the group where they see themselves individually in that diagram. We want to determine if the group collectively understands all aspects of product delivery: can they build the product, will the product lead to the desired outcomes for the customer, and is it a good investment? If a team member understands the costs and the return on investment, the customers' needs, and how to build the product, they are in the intersection of the three circles, right in that sweet spot of the Venn diagram.

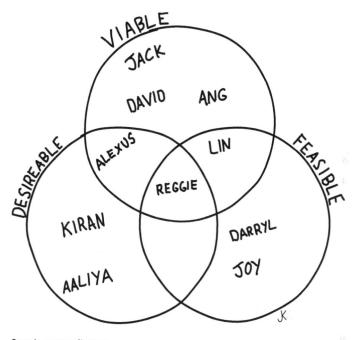

Sample community map

The purpose of this exercise is both to understand the team members' perspectives and to ensure all three perspectives are represented. Having all three perspectives helps us build better products.

The exercise also helps teams understand each other. Different teammates may self-identify in different circles, which often surprises teams. It's an opportunity for teammates to identify the various skills they have and even challenge each other. For example, someone on the team might put themselves squarely in the feasibility circle and someone else on the team will challenge them and say, "Wait a minute. You know a lot about the customer and the product in this case. Shouldn't you be in that part of the diagram where the feasibility and desirability perspectives overlap?"

Many people who come into the dojo identify themselves as having the feasibility perspective—someone involved with the design, construction, and testing of the product—and they enter the dojo with the simple goal of learning a new technical skill. We've had cases where there's been almost no representation from the desirability perspective. When teams see this in their own community maps, it can be a meaningful moment of awareness with far-reaching effects. They may recognize the need to make other people in the organization part of their product development community, or they may decide some people on their team need to take on that perspective. In some cases, it's both. Having these conversations before entering the dojo helps determine if the team comprises the appropriate people and whether any perspectives are missing.

Friendly reminder: don't forget your breaks after every fifty minutes.

BUILDING BETTER PRODUCTS

We had one team that was trying to build a new API for enterprises that were using their network. The new API would allow these enterprises to see their data usage for the month. If they were at risk of an overage, they could use the API to increase their data plan. The team coming into the dojo was building the API to make this information and action possible. When the team first started, they began designing every possible scenario and call the API could support.

If they built everything they thought of, they estimated it would take them six months. Instead, we were able to help them get people who understood the customer involved in the conversation. They said, "If we build a simple API supporting two scenarios, most of our customers would be able to use it right away and we could start making money." The team was able to build an API for those two scenarios in six weeks. They were able to make better decisions and arrive at a better outcome by having the right perspectives involved.

ARCHITECTURE DIAGRAM AND TECH STACK

Teams in the dojo are learning new skills and practices while working on their product. What they can learn is directly related to the architecture and technologies used in their product. As part of chartering, teams create an architecture diagram to get a shared understanding of their architecture and tech stack. Coaches use this visual diagram to help teams explore all the practices they might work on in the dojo, even practices that may be brand-new to them.

The architecture diagram is also used to drive conversations around ensuring teams have access and permissions that will enable them to work on specific practices. For example, if the team wants to learn how to automate deployments, they will need access to the systems that do the deployments. They'll also need permissions that allow them to set up new infrastructure and deploy code to that infrastructure.

Creating the architecture diagram and tech stack starts with the dojo coach asking someone from the team to come to the whiteboard and draw an overview of the architecture for the product. The person may ask to what level of detail the drawing should go. Guide them by letting them know it should at least encompass the systems in play for their product and the technologies that are relevant for their learning. For example, if the team is interested in managing and provisioning systems using the practice of infrastructure as code, then knowing the operating system and other deployment-related details may make sense.

Once the systems and technologies have been added to the diagram, the team highlights the areas they own and have control over. If your product leverages a database, can the team make schema changes, or does it require another group? How does this information and access change what we can learn?

After going through the architecture diagram, you may find out that another team needs to be contacted or permission to access systems or components needs to be granted. This is all good discovery work and will help make for a better learning experience.

DO THIS

- Have someone from the team come up to the whiteboard to draw the architecture.
- They start by placing their system in the center of the whiteboard.
- Ask them to draw/label/write the technologies in play for their system. Have the rest of the team help.
- Ask the group to expand the drawing—who interacts with your system?
- Ask the team if the interactions are direct, or indirect through another system.
- Have the team explain the teams and technologies that are in play for other systems.
- Call out what parts of the architecture the team has direct control over and where they have dependencies on other teams.

- Highlight any questions or options the team wants to explore. The coach offers up ideas for practices that teams have not already identified—chaos engineering, contract testing, and so on.

SKILLS MATRIX

Delivering products requires a multitude of skills, many of which teams don't even think about on a regular basis. With the skills matrix, we are looking to create a way for the team to see all of the skills that they need to have, as a team, to be successful. We use the skills matrix to help define the learning goals for the dojo. We want the team to see that no one knows everything, and we can all teach each other something.

Creating the skills matrix is easy. The coach creates a table on a whiteboard or a large sheet of paper. She then places the name of each team member in a row. She explains to the team that the columns will represent skills. The coach asks the team, "To be successful in our goals, what skills are necessary to have on the team?" As the team mentions skills, the coach fills those in as headers in each column. Have the team refer to the architecture diagram to make sure there is a column for every skill required to develop that architecture.

For example, you can point to the diagram and say, "Over

here you mentioned running Java microservices on a Linux machine. How are you monitoring the service? How are you provisioning the Linux machine? How are you deploying to it?" The skills matrix is not only for technology. Ask teams what skills are needed to understand the product and the customer.

A skills matrix may list twenty to thirty skills—and that is completely normal. The team sees how many skills it takes to deliver a product, and for many, it's the first time they realize how much goes into developing a product.

You then ask each team member to self-identify the skills they can teach and the skills they want to learn. You might use a checkmark for the skills they know well enough to teach and a circle for the skills they want to learn. Leaving it blank is a third option for skills they don't know and don't want to learn, which is okay, because they can't possibly learn everything.

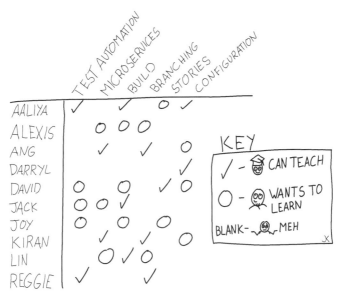

Example skills matrix

Some teams want to add another option: know the skill but can't teach. The challenge with this is the majority of the group will then gravitate to this option because no one wants to admit that they don't know something. Fight this urge to create a fourth option—keep it simple.

Remember, you're trying to visually create a grid that illustrates what the team needs to learn and what skills team members can learn from each other. You want to encourage as much learning within the team as possible. Once the team leaves the dojo, we want continuous learning to be incorporated into the way they work. Helping each other learn new skills will foster continuous learning.

The skills matrix is also used to identify the biggest skills gaps on the team. This is where the dojo coaches will take on responsibility for helping the team upskill.

You might be questioning our use of the word "skills" in this section. Up until now, we've been pretty particular about the use of the words "skills" and "practices." The skills matrix usually ends up being a mixture of skills, specific practices, and, in some cases, tools (e.g., GitLab or AWS CloudFormation templates). From a pragmatic standpoint, that works just fine for defining learning goals.

Friendly reminder: now might be a good time for that final break.

LOGISTICS

Toward the end of the chartering session, the team is typically feeling slightly overwhelmed and drained of energy. Chartering can be mentally taxing, particularly defining the elevator pitch and the goals and success measures. This is a good time to talk about logistics. Logistics are easy to nail down, and the team may feel a sense of accomplishment and excitement after finishing this part of chartering.

Logistics are largely about establishing the team's schedule. You establish the core hours: when the day starts, when it ends, and when the lunch break occurs. Essentially, you're defining when the team will be in the dojo working together; you don't want people coming and going at random times or taking different lunch breaks. We want to maximize the time the team will be learning together.

Most dojos we've worked in use the four core Scrum practices—sprint planning, daily scrum (which we often refer to as a standup), sprint review, and sprint retrospective. Each week in the dojo comprises two sprints, each lasting two-and-a-half days. The coach defines the boundaries of each sprint with the team—the day it begins and the day it ends. The team decides times for the daily scrum, review, and retrospective.

If teams are using a Kanban process, we still recommend they schedule frequent reviews and retrospectives on a regular cadence.

WORKING AGREEMENTS

Usually, teams don't question the way they work together. There is a process they follow without questioning why that process exists or if there are ways of improving it. They may not all even agree on what the process is. As part of chartering, we want the teams to intentionally think about the way they work together. We want them to consider if there are new ways of working together that they want to commit to trying, or at least experimenting with, while they are in the dojo.

For example, maybe the team has been talking about doing code reviews for a year, but they've never implemented them. One of their working agreements could be to require a peer code review before checking in code. Or maybe they've been talking about doing test-driven development but never began practicing it. In the dojo, the team can define that as one of the goals. The working agreement would say that all code written in the dojo will be written using test-driven development.

Some of the agreements may relate to team dynamic issues, such as having group consensus before moving forward on architectural decisions. If stakeholders or leaders are present in the dojo, there may be working agreements the team asks leadership to adhere to, such as not interrupting the team with other requests while they're in the dojo.

In the dojo, we want teams to take these working agreements one step further. We want them to share what they expect to happen with these working agreements—what is the outcome they expect to get from working this way together. For example, if a team agrees that there will be a code review before each commit, they may say that by having this code review, the code will have a more consistent look and design to it. We can then try different approaches to doing code reviews and see if the team feels they are getting the outcomes they had hoped for.

New ways of working together are revisited after the first couple of weeks of the dojo experience. The team and the coach can assess whether or not they are having the desired impact. Adjustments are made as needed.

The working agreements are an opportunity for the team to improve the way they work together. They can use the dojo to establish new habits that will continue when they return to their normal work environment.

SIGNING THE CHARTER

At the end of chartering, everyone on the team, along with the coach, signs the charter they've agreed to. The ritual helps seal the commitment between team members and the dojo. It also gives everyone one last opportunity to voice any concerns or bring up anything they feel wasn't covered.

WHEN IS THE DOJO NOT A GOOD FIT FOR A TEAM?

Not all teams are ready for a dojo experience. The intake process is part of making sure that the team is motivated and prepared for their time in the dojo. Discovering a team isn't a good fit can happen at any point during intake: during the overview, consult, or chartering phase. There are some obvious signs that a team isn't ready to embark on a dojo experience:

- If a team isn't open and willing to commit to learning, it is not the right time for them to enter the dojo.
- If a team has many remote workers who can't come to the shared location for some part of the six weeks, the dojo is not a good fit.
- If a team is not a full-stack, cross-functional team, the dojo is not a good fit. For example, a "team" wants to come into the dojo but they consist only of engineers. There are no testers, designers, or domain experts.
- If a team wants to learn practices and skills the dojo is currently not staffed to teach, the dojo is not a good fit.

Even if you had a good consult with the team, you don't have to take the team into the dojo just because you made it to chartering. Sometimes going through chartering leads to discovering the team would not be a good fit.

You've taken the team through the three phases of intake: overview, consult, and chartering. You've verified the team is a great match for the dojo experience, and they've signed the charter agreement. The team is now ready to begin their dojo experience. The next chapter shows you how to conduct that experience.

Chapter Eight

THE DOJO EXPERIENCE

Programming is a skill best acquired by practice and example rather than from books.

—ALAN TURING, MATHEMATICIAN, COMPUTER
SCIENTIST, LOGICIAN, CRYPTANALYST,
PHILOSOPHER, AND THEORETICAL BIOLOGIST

We went through a smooth intake process with a team, and a week later the team began their six-week dojo experience. We walked into the dojo space with coffee mugs and dry erase markers to find the team already gathered around the whiteboard. One of the architects was drawing the architecture and planning out the code they were going to write that day.

We admired their enthusiasm and self-empowerment, but we interrupted to say, "Before we get into coding, we'll do some practices to help build the backlog. We'll take you through product discovery practices called 'personas' and 'story mapping' to create stories for your product ideas."

They said they already had a backlog of stories. The product owner showed us the spreadsheet she'd brought with her. The stories were high level and not all that great for the work at hand, but we didn't want to make the team duplicate work they'd already done. We asked them to indulge us and go through personas and story mapping for an hour and then decide if we were duplicating previous work.

About fifteen minutes into personas and story mapping, we noticed some murmuring and glances among the team members. We asked what they were thinking. One of the developers said, "You've made us realize that we have no idea what we're building." They all started laughing, including the product owner. They agreed to continue with product discovery, and we ended up working on personas and story maps for three days.

A curious thing happened with this team in the sixth week of their dojo experience. They asked if we could do more product discovery. After they left the dojo, they'd be working on another product effort. The team found product discovery so valuable, they wanted to be sure they understood how to do it on their own when they returned to their normal routine. We observed them go through product discovery, offering corrections where necessary. Because of the dojo's flexible schedule, we were able to respond to the team's specific request on the spot.

THE SIX-WEEK CORE EXPERIENCE

The core dojo experience, and the one we recommend you start with, is six weeks long. We arrived at this duration through experimentation. The reason behind the six weeks is that it's a sufficient duration for people to learn new practices and new ways of working that endure or stick.

Remember, we are battling Ebbinghaus's forgetting curve. Six weeks gives us time to support learning with spaced repetition. In addition, when the experience is shorter than six weeks, the team usually ends up learning practices related to one skill and they don't get the benefit of holistic learning they'd get from a full six-week experience.

In some cases, teams have requested to stay longer than six weeks. We'll extend some dojo experiences to give teams more time for meeting their learning goals, but only toward the end of the scheduled experience. We've found scheduling longer experiences up front leads to a lack of focus and urgency around learning the practices within a reasonable time period. Teams devolve into working the way they normally work. They're just doing it in the dojo space.

REVISITING THE CHARTER

Before beginning to learn any practices on the first day in the dojo, the coaches and team revisit and confirm that the charter everyone signed is still accurate. The coaches ask:

- Has anything changed since we wrote the charter?
- Is this still the problem we're trying to solve?
- Are these still our goals and measures?
- Do you have the answers to any outstanding questions that came up in chartering? For example, if baseline measures were needed, have those been captured? If system access was needed, has access been granted?

This shouldn't take a long time. Sometimes, it takes only five minutes. However, it's worth revisiting the charter to ground the team before we start building the backlog. If there are significant changes to learning or delivery goals, rework the charter to ensure everyone has a shared understanding of what success looks like for the next six weeks.

The charter hangs in a visible spot within the team's space. Keeping the charter in sight serves two purposes:

- Team members refer to it when making decisions to ensure the work they're doing will lead to the desired outcomes.
- It's a visual reminder of previous decisions and a way of externalizing memory so people don't have to keep everything in their heads.

With agreement on the charter, the team moves forward.

BUILDING A BACKLOG

After the team has reviewed their charter, the next step is to build their backlog for the dojo.

For a team focused on new product development, this could involve the creation of personas and story maps. For many team members, this may be the first time they are asked to learn product practices, and product coaching begins here.

It's worth reiterating a point here, since we're starting to talk about the coaching that happens inside the dojo. The dojo doesn't have a predefined curriculum. Coaching is done in the context of the team's real-world work. The product coaching that happens during the first days of the dojo is done in the context of the team's product development.

In our experience, this isn't an issue for experienced product coaches. They may have standard examples they use when teaching new practices, but they're also adept at helping teams apply the practices to real-world products. In addition, product coaches will know contextually which practices to apply in a real-time coaching situation. We've mentioned personas and story maps. Chartering is also a product practice. Those three practices are a minimal set of practices we've used to introduce teams to product thinking. Your product coaches may want to introduce additional practices.

Building the backlog could also involve creating a value stream map of the team's continuous delivery pipeline. Stories can be added to the backlog for work to improve the pipeline based on constraints and problem areas identified in the value stream map. For example, the current pipeline may have manual steps for deployment, and stories can be added to complete that work while learning how to do automated infrastructure setup.

Some teams might be entirely focused on improving technological skills. They might be migrating their applications to the cloud or making improvements to internal platforms and infrastructure. Checklists can be useful in this case. For example, if the team is moving from an Oracle database to a Postgres database, there are known sets of migration tasks that need to be completed (e.g., migrating the schema, migrating the triggers, migrating the data).

In other cases, teams will have to add stories to the backlog by brainstorming about the learning they want to accomplish while they are in the dojo. For the most part, you don't want to add separate stories for learning. The learning should be done in the context of real product development. However, if a team is not doing new development—for example, if they're migrating an application to the cloud—they might need to add stories for refactoring parts of an existing codebase, implementing secure coding practices, or other technical practices. The technical coach can help guide this part of backlog creation.

A team's first story map will show how the product is used to solve a persona's problem, exposing all of the things the team could build.

Teams sometimes get hung up on wanting to perfect the story maps and value stream maps. They don't have to be perfect. As teams start learning practices, they'll understand more about their product and what their continuous delivery pipeline needs to do for them. The maps we create when building the backlog are revisited and updated throughout the six weeks.

In practice, the backlog consists of sticky notes on a whiteboard or wall. The team refers to them as they plan and deliver product features for the remainder of the six weeks. Teams may feel overwhelmed at this point. We emphasize that the backlog reflects possible paths and options. As the team learns, new options will come up and others will be removed. Seeing it visually helps the team make decisions about what to do or not do as they gather information and create knowledge.

Once the team has created their backlog, they are ready to start their first sprint. In some cases, we've been able to move on to sprint planning the afternoon of the first day. Most of the time, the first sprint begins the second or third day. When there is a lot of uncertainty around the product or the technology, it may take the team the entire first week to create their backlog. However, we don't want to start the first sprint any later than Monday of the second week.

SPRINT PLANNING

After we create the initial product backlog, it's time for the team to start their first sprint. The coaches guide the team through sprint planning. Team members might be used to work being divided between individuals and then individuals taking their own tasks. The coaches stress that it's not about what individuals can begin, it's about what the team can complete.

Using the story maps and value streams as a reference, we ask:

- What's the first outcome we want to move toward?
- What's the first thing we want to get done?
- What do we want to learn getting there?

This alleviates some of the overwhelm they may feel when they see the entire backlog. Instead of thinking about all the things they could work on, we ask them to focus on the first outcome they want to achieve. For example, a team might say, "Right now we don't have a way of automatically deploying our code." We say, "Let's take the code you have right now and make it so it can automatically be deployed." Together, we define the first outcome as automatically deployed code to some kind of environment, and we put that in a lane in the story map labeled "Now."

We then ask the team, "For that outcome, what's the simplest set of things from the backlog we need to do?" We move those sticky notes up on the whiteboard, and they become the things to do to get to the "Now" outcome.

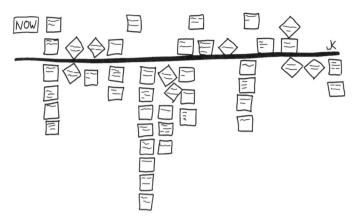

Teams choose a first outcome, and then move related stories in the map up to a "Now" section.

The next question is "If we complete that outcome, what's our next best investment?" This phrase encourages them to think about both the technical and product side of things, because sometimes they need to invest in exploratory activities. We write "Next" on the story map and then identify the things from the backlog that support that "Next" outcome. Everything else is considered "Later."

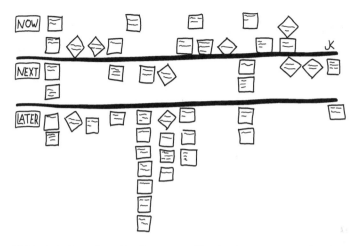

Finished plan for sprints with a first outcome (Now) and second outcome (Next) defined. Minimal stories needed for those outcomes are placed in the respective swimlanes, with the remainder in a "Later" section.

We want teams to shift their focus to outcomes rather than individual stories. We help them get an idea of what's in the "Next" category but emphasize that "Next" might change. To summarize, the teams focus on this kind of preliminary planning and answer three questions:

- What's our next best investment?
- What's the next outcome you want to produce?
- What do we need to do and learn to get there?

As the teams go through their sprints, we repeat this exercise. When a team finishes a sprint, we ask if they reached the first outcome. If so, great. If they were not able to meet that outcome—and, early on, this will happen—we ask them what we learned and what we need to adjust in our plan. This information is then included in our backlog and we decide if our "Next" is still appropriate or if we need to invest more in the previous outcome that was missed.

For example, a team's first outcome might have been to automatically deploy their code to a development environment. While trying to learn deployment automation and deliver this outcome, the team learned that they had some code dependencies that were not properly being tracked, leading to misconfigured environments. They discuss this and add the dependency management work to their backlog. The team then decides if they want to continue trying to get the code automatically deployed or if there is a different best investment right now. We then ask the preliminary planning questions again to identify a new "Next" outcome.

TWO-AND-A-HALF-DAY SPRINTS

If we begin a sprint on Wednesday, we ask the team if they can finish the outcome by Friday, because we're working in two-and-a-half-day increments. It's radically simpler for people to grasp two-and-a-half days than two weeks, a standard sprint length for many Agile teams. If the outcome is too big to complete in two-and-a-half days, we break it down to a smaller, simpler outcome. If the outcome is too big, the question isn't "What tasks do we remove," but rather "What is a simpler outcome that we feel confident we can achieve?"

The dojo isn't about making sure people are as busy as possible, but rather that the team is achieving their learning goals and getting to the right outcomes.

Within the six-week dojo experience, we're able to have eleven or twelve sprints. This gives teams the opportunity to practice the skills of planning, executing, doing demos, and holding retrospectives. They also practice "getting to done."

As we mentioned before, the two-and-a-half-day sprints provide a margin of psychological safety. If a team goes down a rabbit hole or does something that ends up not being right, they've only spent two-and-a-half days doing it. Learning often happens best when we fail at something. The short sprints provide plenty of opportunity for failure and learning, and there's time to course correct when the team plans the next sprint.

WHY TWO-AND-A-HALF DAYS?

We've written a blog post to answer this question.[1] In a nutshell, there are six reasons:

- Repetition fosters learning.
- Teams practice getting to done.
- Teams (finally) learn how to break stories down into doable-size tasks.
- Learning is supported by a margin of safety.
- Frequent retrospectives lead to the proper mindset.
- There are more opportunities to ask "What is the next best investment in learning?"

ADJUSTING LEARNING GOALS ALONG THE WAY

Learning goals are adjusted on a continuous basis. The coaches meet the teams where they are and help the teams learn new practices based on what's happening in real time. This is critical to note: some organizations will ask for and expect a curriculum when starting a dojo. Your response is that the dojo is not one size fits all. It is dynamic and responds in real time to where teams are on their learning journey.

---

1   "Six Reasons Why We Do Two-and-a-Half-Day Sprints in the Dojo," *Dojo and Co.* (blog), December 8, 2017, https://www.dojoandco.com/blog/2017/12/8/six-reasons-why-we-do-two-and-a-half-day-sprints-in-the-dojo.

Technical practices have been marginalized for far too long. In the dojo it's important for the technical coaches to ensure teams are developing their technical skills with a deep understanding of what's happening with the technology. We've worked with extremely intelligent engineers who sometimes try to brute force their way through problems without developing an understanding of the technology involved.

For example, teams commonly use Maven to manage builds on Java projects. We've seen engineers encounter problems and repeatedly run the "clean" and "install" commands in an effort to get the build to run. They don't take the time to fully understand why the build isn't working properly. Sometimes they never had the time to learn how Maven works. Someone else on their team set up the Maven build, and they just run the commands. Not understanding Maven builds is one thing, but imagine the problems that could result if engineers are spinning up services in the cloud without a deep understanding of what they are doing.

The dojo is about learning over delivery. Teams need to be given time to slow down and learn technology and technical practices without the pressure of meeting some arbitrary learning deadline.

In the same way that product coaches help teams learn

practices by applying them to their own products, technical coaches help teams learn by applying practices to their real-world work. Rather than relying on standard examples or exercises, technical coaches look for opportunities to teach techniques and practices as they are working with the team. For example, if a team is learning how to refactor their legacy codebase so they can start writing automated tests for it, the coach will look for opportunities to teach refactoring techniques in the team's codebase. They'll ask the team to identify a section of the code they want to test and work with the team to refactor it to a point where tests can be written, making sure the team understands the refactoring techniques as they go.

Technical coaches don't have to figure out exactly what people need to learn. The work itself will provide opportunities for the team to learn what they need to learn. Again, there's no need for a predefined curriculum. (Entire volumes have been written about technical practices. There's no need to rewrite them.) The dojo provides a safe learning environment and, as long as a coach has skills in the practices they are helping the team with, the learning will happen.

Having said all that, it may be useful to see an example of what teams might learn during a week in a dojo.

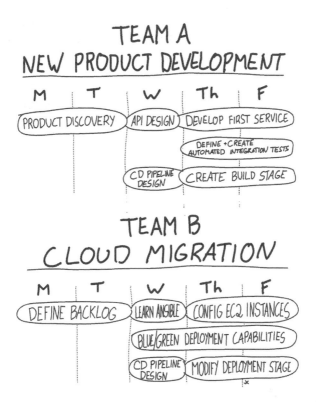

An example of what teams might learn over the course of a week

In the first few sprints, it's common for the whole team to gather around a TV or large monitor to participate in mob programming sessions. In the past, it was common to have developers work in pairs. Working as a whole team is a newer way of working and learning. (*Mob Programming: A Whole Team Approach* by Woody Zuill and Kevin Meadows[2] explains this way of working in detail.)

---

2 K. Meadows and W. Zuill, *Mob Programming: A Whole Team Approach* (Leanpub, 2016), http://leanpub.com/mobprogramming.

We've found mob programming to be an effective tool for helping teams learn new practices.

After a week or two, the team can decide if they want to continue working this way or if they want to work in smaller groups. If the team decides to work in smaller groups, they'll still come together and use the monitor to do whole-team learning and sharing once or twice a day.

Around the third week, the team starts doing their own sprint planning, daily standups, demos, and retros. Some teams already have a scrum master who leads these practices when they come into the dojo. In other cases, one of the team members emerges as a scrum master. If that doesn't happen, another option is for the team to rotate that responsibility.

The learning becomes more self-directed. The technical coach remains hands-on in weeks three and four as the team puts the skills they've learned in weeks one and two into practice. The product coach and Agile coach encourage the team to take on more responsibility for themselves and move into more of a supporting role, answering questions as they come up and making course corrections as necessary.

Over the course of six weeks, the coaches' role and time with the team diminishes. Early on, the coaches are heavily involved—teaching, facilitating, and guiding the team's learning. The goal over the course of the six weeks is for the team to become more self-sufficient in owning their learning. This way, when the team leaves the dojo, the learning and growth continues. This can only happen if the coaches do not become a crutch.

In the last two weeks, teams are fully using the skills and practices, with little input from the coaches. The goal of the dojo is for teams to adopt a way of working and learning on their own, although coaches remain available to answer questions and offer assistance.

The dojo teaches teams to be continuous learners in a learning organization.

STANDUPS, DEMOS, AND RETROSPECTIVES

Each morning, the team has a standup. The team shares what they've learned and any interesting discoveries about getting to their planned outcome. They also talk about whether anything needs to be done differently, or if obstacles block the work. The dojo standup is about the team learning, not about what tasks each individual is completing.

The demo happens at the end of each two-and-a-half-day sprint. The team shows the increment of the product or pipeline that was developed over the last two-and-a-half days, sharing what practices they learned along the way. You want the team to be explicit about what they've learned over those two-and-a-half days, because the dojo is about learning within the context of delivery. For example, if they learned something about building their pipeline or doing architecture in the cloud, you want them to talk about that. The team will start off the demo telling the audience the outcome they were working toward and what they learned along the way getting there. Then, the team shows the work completed, asking and answering questions along the way.

The person who leads the demo rotates every time, regardless of title or role.

Encourage your leaders at the manager, director, and executive levels to engage with the dojo as much as possible so they can ask questions and talk about their concerns. The most common concerns tend to focus on time—why is this taking so long? Dojo staff can have candid conversations with leaders about what happens in the dojo, so the team doesn't feel intimidated by leadership.

One effective way of getting leaders engaged is to have them attend demos. When the team recounts their progress, leaders and stakeholders can witness for themselves the benefits of continuous learning. Additionally, when the team explains the friction and confusion they encountered while trying to deliver an outcome, good leadership makes note of this and works to resolve the friction. A good leader makes it easier for their teams and people to succeed.

At the end of the sprint, teams do a retrospective and ask themselves:

- What's working well that's supporting our learning?
- What's inhibiting our learning?
- Is there anything we want to try differently to support our learning over the next few days? If we try something different, what do we expect will happen? What is the benefit we want from trying these changes to how we learn?

We encourage teams to pick one new improvement to try each sprint. With a sprint length of two-and-a-half days, it's difficult to implement more than one change at a time.

WEEKLY WRAP-UP

At the end of every week in the dojo, the dojo coaches write a one-page bulleted summary with four sections:

- The team's and coaches' planned goals for the week

- What we were able to accomplish and what we learned along the way. If there's a delta, we explain why the delta exists.
- Things we plan to do the following week, in light of what we did
- Learnings about the organization as a whole, such as constraints or things that block the team from completing their learnings or delivering their product

The weekly reports are distributed to the teams, leadership for the teams, and the leadership and stakeholders for the dojo itself. Use the reports to engage team leaders and get their help removing constraints impeding the teams' learning. In some cases, the constraints will need to be fixed at an organizational level. We talk about this more in chapter 10.

The dojo experience impacts how teams learn and work together. When the six weeks ends, most teams are enthusiastic about taking newly learned—and ingrained—practices back to their day-to-day work routine. Their new ways of working empower them to solve problems as they arise and work more effectively. In the next chapter, we look at ways of supporting teams after they leave the dojo.

Chapter Nine

POST-DOJO FOLLOW-UP

I never am really satisfied that I understand anything; because, understand it well as I may, my comprehension can only be an infinitesimal fraction of all I want to understand about the many connections and relations which occur to me, how the matter in question was first thought of or arrived at, etc., etc.

—ADA LOVELACE, MATHEMATICIAN AND
CONTRIBUTOR TO THE ANALYTICAL ENGINE

We decided to check in on the POS (point of sale) team unannounced. It had been about two months since they'd completed their dojo experience. While they were in the dojo, they had called themselves the Eliminators because one of their goals was to replace a vendor's library with their own code. We'd heard they'd recently met this goal and wanted to congratulate the team.

The first thing we noticed when we got to their team space was the overall mood. Everyone seemed happy and they all smiled when they noticed us. It seemed like a different team from when we'd first met them.

We asked them how things were going, and they told us their time in the dojo helped them think about small, continuous improvements without getting overwhelmed. They were able to carry this thinking into their day-to-day work and it helped them remove the vendor library. They were also continuing to expand the number of tests in their automated test suites. We had started this work in the dojo.

The team said they still had one big problem and didn't know how to solve it. Each store had different data sets used for coupons and payment structures. The testing around those varied data sets was hard, and the team didn't know a good way to create the test data. They had automated creating new database instances, and they loaded test data using SQL scripts, but the automation was taking a long time to run. The data had to be reset every time the code was tested. In their minds, the cycle time was still too long for testing, fixing defects, and validating the fixes.

We spent about half an hour talking with them about creating "golden master" binary snapshots of their database once the test data had been loaded. We had learned about this technique at a lecture given by Peter Schuh about fifteen years ago. (You can read about this technique in Schuh's white paper, "Agility and the Database."[1]) We talked about how they should be able to get their database setup time down to under a minute using the binary snapshot and how they could update the binary snapshot over time and check it into version control so that it would always be in sync with the current codebase.

About a week later, a few of their team members stopped by the dojo to tell us they'd implemented the database snapshot technique. The testers loved it. They were able to reset test environments in a matter of minutes, and the team as a whole was able to fix defects and verify the fixes in minutes and hours instead of days. They also knew that if they got stuck on anything going forward, they could reach out to the dojo as a resource for thinking through strategies and solutions.

CONTINUOUS IMPROVEMENT

Teams can make significant improvements by learning new practices and skills. We've seen teams make radical improvements in the six weeks they spend in a dojo. However, the real impact comes when teams adopt a mindset

---

1   Peter Schuh, "Agility and the Database," *ResearchGate*, June 2002, https://www.researchgate. net/publication/2523742_Agility_and_the_Database.

of continuous learning and improvement. When this happens, and this mindset starts taking hold across multiple teams, that's when real organizational change happens.

Our industry uses the word "transformation" too much. We talk about Agile transformations, DevOps transformations, and product model transformations. The word itself implies a specific endpoint—the transformation will be done when some ideal end state has been reached. In our careers, we've even fielded questions around how much these transformations cost and what other organizations are paying to get to this ideal end state.

What we should be talking about is continuous transformation, or evolution. Teams need to learn how to incorporate continuous improvement and learning into the way they work on a daily basis. Only then will organizations become learning organizations, able to compete in today's rapidly changing business environment.

Going back to our POS team. When we first met them, they were frustrated and stuck in a rut. They were some of the best engineers we'd met, but they'd inherited a legacy system that was a mess. Prior to the team's formation, any changes to the C++ codebase had been outsourced to the cheapest bidder. This had gone on for twenty years. There was bad code written on top of bad code.

In a typical week, the engineers delivered a build to the testing team on Friday. The testing team tested nonstop for five days, until the next build came. They never had a chance to invest in test automation because they were always chasing their tail.

Engineers were trying to write good code over bad. The team's scrum master and managers tried to provide helpful guidance. They'd say, "You should do Agile. You should do Scrum. You should start doing test-driven development and you should automate the QA tests." But that never helped.

By the time they reached the dojo, these super-smart engineers had reached their breaking point and were both suspicious and hesitant to work with us. They said, "We've heard this story before. You're going to tell us we need test automation. We know we need to do this, but it's hard."

Instead, we took a different approach to the problem. First, we looked at what they were working on and agreed the code was a mess. We weren't judging them. We were sympathetic to the situation they were in. We acknowledged that no one could wave their hand over the keyboard and magically solve the problem. We explained that, in the dojo, we would first come up with a strategy, then attack the problem together. With this approach, we diffused their skepticism and frustration and began to build trust with the engineers.

We helped them change their mindset, so they could get into the practice of continuously taking small steps to make the code better. We asked them to create a list of all the things they wanted to do to improve the code, and then broke that list into the smallest pieces possible. While working on those small improvements, we taught them techniques for adding tests to legacy codebases. After the first week, they could see progress. Their mantra shifted from "It's too hard. It's too hard" to "What is the next smallest step we can take to improve this codebase?"

The test-driven development and legacy code refactoring practices we worked on with the team were important for the team's success. However, the most significant thing we accomplished with this team was helping them adopt the mindset of continuous learning and improvement. That mindset stuck with the team even after they left the dojo.

We recommend that every dojo defines one of its outcomes as helping teams adopt a mindset of continuous learning and improvement.

PREPPING TEAMS FOR CONTINUED SUCCESS

Sit down with the team a week before they leave the dojo to have an exit interview. The coaches have been with the team for five weeks by this point, and a deep sense of trust has developed. We like to ask teams, "Is there anything you're worried about, now that you're leaving and going back to your normal workspace? What can we do to help you?" The responses from the team tend to be honest.

You want to learn what the team found most valuable and what they want to take back to their normal work environment. Ask them what they plan to learn next. You want teams to always be thinking about the next learning opportunity, the next improvement they'll work on. You want them to take the continuous learning mindset with them.

You want to ensure that when teams return to their own workspace and routines, they can continue the practices that they started learning in the dojo and are able to continue the collaborative ways of working together that you've helped them adopt. You also want to make sure they understand the idea of continuous learning and improvement. It's not enough to simply replicate the practices and collaboration as they did in the dojo; they should be empowered to face new challenges and continue to build their skills on their own.

Some concerns the teams have are easily solved, and the dojo staff can create a big impact with a small change. For example, before the dojo experience, some teams worked in different areas and didn't have access to whiteboards for product design and discussion. The team may express the desire to have whiteboards in their team space after they leave the dojo. If the dojo staff can help make this happen, this simple change can have a big impact for the team. They'll feel motivated to continue working as they did in the dojo and bring some of the dojo vibe into their regular workspace.

Other teams worry about distractions. They say, "The biggest thing we're worried about is getting pulled in four directions." The dojo product manager can talk to leadership and say, "Remember how the team was working before they came in? They were thrashing around trying to get multiple things done at once, and the system was unstable. We showed them some technical practices and techniques for being more focused in their work, and systems and deployments started to get better. Now they're concerned that after leaving the dojo they'll be pulled in different directions because of misaligned priorities, undoing the stability they have started to create. How do we help the team not have these kinds of fears?"

You can support and defend the team when the change

that will help them most is something leadership or a group outside the team has to make.

ONGOING FOLLOW-UP

Whether the worries are big or small, you're trying to figure out a way to make sure the team will be successful going forward.

When the coaches conduct the exit interview, they set up a cadence for check-ins. (Operations managers sometimes attend the exit interviews and add the check-ins to everyone's calendars.) You want the team to know that you're there to support them. Agree to a cadence that works for them. Some coaches check in after the first week, then after a month, and every two months after that. When you do check in, ask which practices stuck and what challenges arose after leaving the dojo—and don't forget to ask how you can help them again.

You can schedule formal check-in meetings, but *informal* check-ins often provide more accurate information. People tend to say everything's great in formal check-ins. When you stop by their workspace or show up during a standup, you observe what's really happening.

You may sit in on a team's standup and notice that they've stopped focusing on their team outcomes and instead are focusing on individual tasks. Or they had design discussions as a group in the dojo, then fell back on assigning tasks to individuals without first having design discussions. You want to find out what happened and how you can help them to regain what they learned and practiced in the dojo.

Stop by a team's demo. This allows you to ask questions such as "I see that you're still using questions to gain deeper knowledge in the demo rather than just showing status, like we did in the dojo. How is this still valuable for you?" Find out what they've continued to use and what practices they've modified to better suit themselves. If they have changed practices from how they did them in the dojo, ask why they changed. Some teams change with good reason, others fall back on old habits because they can't figure out how to recreate what they did in the dojo. You may not learn these things if you set up a formal check-in.

Informal check-ins give you a chance to see if you can help the teams in any way after they leave the dojo. Some teams realize there's more to learn and want to return to the dojo. While the first dojo experience is six weeks, you can set up a shorter-duration dojo experience for a returning team that desires specific learning.

You want the team to feel supported, and you want to reinforce the idea of continuous improvement and learning. You also want to make sure the changes they experienced become permanent and valuable to them. If the practices learned in the dojo remain in the dojo, the experience has failed. The goal is for teams to learn how to work together effectively after they leave the dojo.

MEASURING THE DOJO'S IMPACT

In chapter 3, we encouraged you to define the outcomes and impacts you want your dojo to have on your organization. We encouraged you to do this even before you thought about the specific practices and skills you want teams to learn in your dojo. Part of assessing how well your dojo is working is to see how well teams are doing once they've left the dojo. In addition, you'll want to see what kind of impact the dojo is having on the organization as a whole.

This is primarily a matter of capturing and reporting on metrics at the organizational level. For example, if your goal was to reduce operating costs by migrating applications to the cloud, you'll want to continuously capture metrics on the number of applications you've helped teams migrate, as well as operating costs in the cloud versus operating costs when you were running the applications in your own data centers.

Most likely, you'll have to gather metrics from multiple

places. You may have tools that measure code quality as part of your continuous delivery pipelines. You may have to use your planning and tracking tools to measure delivery cycle times. Other tools may have to be tapped to gather metrics around successful versus failed deployments. You get the picture.

What you don't want to do, however, is implement only simple organizational reach metrics that include the number of teams that have gone through your dojo. Slightly better would be the number of teams implementing a specific practice. But even then, so what? Who cares if forty teams have learned how to automate their infrastructure deployment? What *impact* is that having at the organizational level?

We can't stress enough the importance of defining your high-level outcomes and the impact you want to have on the organization. When you do that, defining and capturing metrics that show the value of your dojo becomes possible. Without doing that, you may be confused about what metrics you want to capture, and you may find yourself scrambling to prove the value of your dojo. You might even find yourself at risk of having your dojo shut down.

Obviously, if the metrics you're capturing don't indicate you're having the desired impact on your organization, you'll need to make adjustments. This could come in the form of changing the practices you teach, bringing in additional coaches with different skills, and modifying your offerings. If you find yourself in this situation, pull your dojo staff together and work through ideas for making improvements as a team.

You may also find there are constraints impacting teams' ability to make improvements that are beyond their control to handle. The constraints may be at the organizational level, not at the team level. The next chapter explains how to leverage the dojo for continuous learning and improvement at the organizational level.

Chapter Ten

LEVERAGING DOJOS THROUGHOUT THE ORGANIZATION

Humans are allergic to change. They love to say, "We've always done it this way." I try to fight that. That's why I have a clock on my wall that runs counter-clockwise.

—GRACE HOPPER, COMPUTER SCIENTIST AND
UNITED STATES NAVY REAR ADMIRAL

As soon as teams begin going through the dojo experience, cracks in an organization's veneer begin to show. Problems arise for teams when the organization—often without awareness—imposes constraints on the team that keep the team from functioning at its best.

The first team that came into the dojo in a large enterprise was composed of people who usually worked on four different teams. We brought this team in, and they were learning new skills and practices: product thinking, Agile practices, test-driven practices, pipelines, and so forth. We quickly encountered visible constraints that weren't the team's issues, but rather the organization's issues.

Prior to coming to the dojo, and even for the first couple of weeks inside the dojo, two individuals on the same team, a front-end engineer and a middleware engineer, were never allowed to see each other's code—code that works together seamlessly to the end user. If either of their code is not working, the product is not usable. The company had hired and trusted these individuals to build two parts of the same product (front-end/back-end), yet they weren't trusted to see each other's code.

The reason? Default security policies. As far as we could tell, there were no valid security reasons for locking down visibility to the code.

This type of mistrust results in fragile systems where people make guesses about how components work because it takes too long to find the answer to a question. When team members can't see the code their code interacts with, they start making logical assumptions about how it works, and defects can arise from there.

Unfortunately, this scenario is more common than it is

rare. In their day-to-day work outside the dojo, these team members lived with that friction all the time. The front-end engineer couldn't see what was happening on the back end. She didn't sit by the team member writing the back-end code, so she had to send an email or make guesses about how her code would interact with the middleware engineer's code. These friction points become clear when teams begin working in the dojo.

FRICTION POINTS

It seems obvious that these friction points shouldn't exist when teams work on the same product. The organization unwittingly creates impediments and often isn't aware of them, because everyone is busy doing so many things all the time. Waiting on someone? Just start something else. Efficiency over effectiveness.

Once the whole team comes into the dojo space and focuses on learning and finishing things together, organizational constraints blow up quickly. The organization, as long as it's prepared for this, learns what constraints are preventing their teams from delivering value.

Most organizations, however, aren't prepared.

When we document the friction points and share them with leadership, the initial reaction is often "The team has plenty to do. If they run into a constraint, they can put that work on hold until that constraint is addressed, and work on other things in the meantime." Leaders believe the pervasive myth that you don't lose efficiency by switching tasks, when in fact the statistics are quite astounding. In *Quality Software Management, Volume 1: Systems Thinking*, Gerald Weinberg calculates that adding a second project to your workload is profoundly debilitating; you lose 20 percent of your time. By the time you add a third project to the mix, nearly half your time is wasted in task switching.[1] Working on a second task while waiting for missing pieces of the first task appears to be an efficient use of time, but clearly it's an ineffective practice.

In the opening scenario, the front-end engineer started tracking how much time she was losing because she didn't have access to the back-end code. Her data showed 20 percent of her time was lost to security policies: not being able to see teammates' code, not being able to debug environments, and—absurdly—not being able to access documentation for frameworks used in their development because of where the documentation was hosted. A year and a half later, security finally said, "Wow, this is actually a big problem." We learned this inside the dojo, but it had to be solved at an organization level.

---

1   Gerald Weinberg, *Quality Software Management Volume 1: Systems Thinking.* (New York: Dorset House, 1992).

Friction points come in many forms, but there are several that we've consistently seen in most organizations: silo challenges (like the example above), compliance issues, architectural flaws, delivery bias, poor technical practices, and documentation substituting for good processes. We'll explore each of these in the following pages.

SILO CHALLENGES

You'd think in 2019 silos would no longer exist inside organizations. Sadly, they do. Governance and security often keep the ideation, delivery, and operations teams separate.

It shouldn't have to take a dojo to point out the inherent problems when development and quality assurance (QA) are divided. We see organizational patterns repeated over and over where these two groups (development and QA) are completely different teams managed by different people. For example, testing is hard because development engineers don't have good design practices and create systems that are not designed to be tested in isolation from each other. Organizations then create a test-data management team to coordinate setting up data across multiple systems for the testing teams, but the testing folks and the test-data management folks don't talk to each other, nor to the development team—the ones that could actually make testing easier. For the tester to do any testing, she has to request a reload from a test-data team.

More recently, we see this separation in organizations that have a newly formed "DevOps" team. This team is, in all reality, automated infrastructure. Developers cannot create, access, or deploy to their environments, but the DevOps team can. And they are expected to do it for everyone. Meet the new boss, same as the old boss.

One of the most common silos in organizations is the separation between ideation (the product) and engineering. As we know, having better product context—a rich understanding of the customer and deep knowledge about the problems we are trying to solve—results in better product delivery. And understanding the constraints of the systems helps guide what is feasible for a product. The dojo looks to break down these silos and challenge the idea that product thinking happens only outside of IT.

You may have experienced something like this: an engineer we were working with received a requirement to add more data to a web page, because "the business said so." Adding more data is easy. But is it helpful? We asked the engineer to dig into the request and gain understanding about why the additional data was needed. It turned out more data would have actually been confusing—what was really needed was to clarify what was already being presented.

Ironically, organizations often create silos in the name

of efficiency, but they end up hampering the flow of value delivery. A dojo helps organizations build product communities who own their product delivery start to finish, from ideation through operating and running in production.

COMPLIANCE ISSUES

Compliance laws, such as Sarbanes-Oxley or HIPAA, create multiple constraints. To make matters worse, organizations use fear of compliance to block people from doing certain activities without actually understanding the compliance rules.

We often work with organizations that want to adopt DevOps to automate deployments. We begin talking to the team in the consult or chartering part of intake and they say, "We're not allowed to automate deployment because I'm not allowed to have access to the production systems because of Sarbanes-Oxley."

Every organization gets audited for SOX (Sarbanes-Oxley) compliance. A random auditor looks at how you manage your systems and makes arbitrary decisions, because SOX compliance is nebulous at best, especially as technology changes. Security reads what the auditors say and makes their own interpretation around the policies that are in play. One client's security team told us,

"Engineers cannot do their own builds and they cannot deploy their own code in any environment." To support their security decision, a new team was spun up. It was called the release engineering team. This team wasn't writing code, but when the engineers finished writing code, they told the release engineers to build the code and deploy it to the various environments for them. Only the release engineers, who didn't write the code, were permitted to build the code and deploy it to the environments. The company called it a "separation of concerns," which is interpreted as "if you're building it, you shouldn't know how it runs." This presents a cyclical problem because the release engineers don't have the context the builders do, and the builders don't have the context for how the release engineers are deploying code.

If the compliance people had spoken with the engineers, they would have discovered there's a fully automated, traceable, auditable approach to doing deployments where the engineers don't touch the systems. It's actually more effective and easier to trace and audit from a compliance perspective. Automated deployment adheres more to the spirit of Sarbanes-Oxley than one individual with elevated privileges deploying manually. Unfortunately, most people don't understand the rules.

ARCHITECTURE FLAWS

After you work with a few teams, you start to see common anti-patterns or problems with the systems architecture. Often, the teams are simply used to working around the problems, accepting the current architecture as a constraint. A deployment that has to be done in a certain order due to bad coupling of components is an example of an architecture that is the constraint. If you have five teams working on a product and all five teams spend large amounts of time coordinating their changes and deployment, the architecture is very likely the cause. In some cases, teams might not know what modern architectures could look like and how things could be improved.

In many organizations, teams don't think about architecture in the rush to get work done. They end up duplicating effort, data, services, systems, or capabilities over and over again. They don't think about how the architecture could support the needs of the many. Teams then create special APIs or single-use database views or, more commonly, repeat code and make one small change. They have a build-and-deploy process that only works for their team. This leads to unnecessary complexity because the architecture hasn't evolved with the needs of the product.

We had one organization where over ten different teams committed to the same codebase. On top of that, there were no tests. There was no modularity in the code, which would help teams work more independently. While we could work with the individual teams, the largest constraint was the architecture. Helping address this constraint would then enable practices around testing and deployment for all of the teams.

PRODUCT THINKING VERSUS DELIVERY BIAS

"Product thinking" is the mindset teams use to understand the problem they're trying to solve and the outcomes they're trying to obtain, as opposed to thinking only about the systems and technology they're trying to deliver. Many organizations have "delivery bias" and believe that as long as they deliver more stuff, they'll be successful.

Dojos tend to show that often the things teams are building aren't having the impact the teams expected.

Delivery teams are often viewed as order takers, delivering according to the specs that someone else creates. A dojo challenges that mentality. It pulls in business subject matter experts, product managers, and people who know the product domain. In a dojo, the entire team operates as a more cohesive community that's focused on delivering a product that serves an actual customer need.

What's more, a dojo can provide baseline metrics to

measure whether what you're doing is used or is solving customers' problems. If a team is introducing a feature they believe will increase sales, we establish concrete goals for increasing sales during chartering. We also establish how we will measure sales. Once the feature is delivered, we continually track the measurements to see if the feature has the impact on sales we expected.

The focus shifts away from delivering output (e.g., number of features) to delivering value.

FINALLY ADDRESSING TECHNICAL PRACTICES

Agile methodologies were created in the 1990s. All of them call out the need for both process improvements and technical practice improvements. Many organizations have only paid lip service to the technical practices because they're harder to implement, and not everyone who pushes for Agile transformations understands the technical practices. The dojo stresses the importance of technical practices, not only for helping build systems with technical quality, but as the foundation that allows you to learn about your product in a consistent manner. Weak technical practices lead to fragile systems and rework—all of which take away from your ability to learn more about your customers and your products.

Many organizations use sophisticated tools for building

their products. As a result, they believe they're doing well with the technical practices. They don't realize that the behaviors and practices to use the tools effectively aren't in place. For example, they might be using Git for source code control. But instead of having a defined branching strategy, or at least having minimal sets of branches and frequently checking in code, they have long running branches and code everywhere in a distributed mess. They'll talk about test code coverage, but they don't realize that they actually have fragile tests that don't make developers feel confident when making changes.

When teams come into a dojo, they'll often admit they're using certain tools but that they know they don't understand how to use them well. They're using them because they have to or because they're the only tools available to them. A dojo will quickly reveal when an organization hasn't focused on its technical practices.

DOCUMENTED DOESN'T MEAN USEFUL

When a team begins a dojo experience, we'll often ask how they currently do things, like spin up a server in the cloud. Someone will say, "Well, it's already documented. Just go read the documents." We'll read it and try for a day, then point out the problems we found. We're often told we read an outdated document and are given a different one to read. We try again, and the same thing happens.

Teams often believe if they write down all the steps for accomplishing a specific task, everybody will understand how it's done. One person knows how to deploy something, he writes it down, and has now given it to the masses. Just because one person had that one experience, doesn't mean that somebody else can read through it, follow along, and have the same experience. Again, the dojo focuses on experience-based learning, because we know learning sticks best through doing—knowledge creation over knowledge transfer.

That's not to say practices shouldn't be documented; they should. We encourage teams to make their own living documents, keeping in mind who will read the document and why. We encourage teams to "test" the documentation by having others work through it. When the documentation "fails," we encourage the teams to treat it like a failing test case in a build. The first priority is to fix the documentation. If the team is not treating the documentation with this level of diligence, is the documentation really valuable?

What's more, well-documented processes aren't necessarily good processes. We worked with one group whose teams had to answer 104 risk-assessment questions to get approval to begin work on a new project. A team would take four days to navigate the 104 questions, getting most of them wrong. The whole process was flaky, but it was documented. We found that a team could have a "risk engineer" who would spend a few minutes with the team during chartering, ask a few questions, and then say, "Yep, sounds good."

In another organization, it took four weeks to get a new firewall rule implemented. If a team is spending six weeks in a dojo, four weeks waiting for a new firewall rule is an eternity that severely impedes their progress. When we inquired about the firewall process, we were told it was a well-known, well-documented process.

The fact that these processes were well documented is pointless.

Processes end up this way because something bad happened years ago. Information gets leaked or a system crashes and the knee-jerk reaction is to add another step to a process to ensure that it never happens again. We believe it's far better to educate the people who contributed to the problem in the first place. Dojos are a way of accomplishing this. You're not going to process your way into being a world-class product development organization. You've got to invest in the education of the people doing the work.

WORKING WITH LEADERS

A dojo helps product development teams adopt a continuous learning mindset, which empowers them to solve problems and create new knowledge during the course of their work. A dojo also impacts the management in an organization. The dojo works with two levels of leaders: the direct managers of the teams inside the dojo and the executives above them.

The dojo will be challenging for the direct team leaders. If they're used to checking in, controlling the team as well as the process, and making decisions about deliverables, they'll feel separated and concerned about the pace and their own lack of control. It may be strange for them to see the team making their own decisions.

The dojo staff has to be prepared to support direct managers during their team's dojo experience. Ideally, direct managers are involved in the consult and chartering and participate in scheduled weekly check-ins, so they can voice any concerns they have and get direct information and feedback from the coach about what the team is learning. Their involvement throughout their team's dojo experience provides them with the information they need to feel comfortable with what's happening. It's important for the dojo staff to be both a voice and an ear for direct managers.

ADDRESSING FRICTION POINTS

You won't be able to address these types of friction by working only with the teams inside the dojo. You'll have to make connections with people in security roles, enterprise architecture groups, the project management office (PMO), and product management. The first step in addressing the constraints is making sure everyone is aware of them and the impact they are having on teams' ability to deliver.

The dojo staff create backlogs for organizational constraints that they'd like to help the organization remove. They form working groups with partners from outside the dojo and start working through the items in the backlog the same way teams work through items in their backlogs. Coaches with downtime between teams may be able to help work through backlog items. In other cases, you'll have to get buy-in from your partners to get them to change their policies and processes. You might even have to get senior leadership involved to help drive changes.

If you followed the suggestions in this book, you defined outcomes you want your dojo to help your organization achieve as the first step in creating your dojo. If you can provide evidence showing how organizational constraints are impeding your ability to achieve those outcomes, you'll have an easier time making the case for change and getting support from senior leadership.

CONCLUSION

The best time to plant a tree was twenty years ago. The second best time is now.

—CHINESE PROVERB

KEEPING THE DOJO RELEVANT

To keep the dojo relevant, you need to revisit your original goals and measures to make sure they're still valid. The dojo is a product, and you treat it as such. Over the course of time, you'll receive feedback and learn about the needs of your organization. You can then evolve your offerings as you learn. Start simple, with the standard six-week dojo offering. Once that is up and running well, consider if you should provide custom-designed offerings based upon the new needs of your organization and your teams.

In some organizations, teams start going through the dojo experience and the dojo staff learn there's a lot of interest in doing deeper product exploration. The dojo then creates a new offering to do two weeks of product exploration. It's still a dojo and it's still the team's work, but they'll learn more involved product-exploration tools in a different part of the value stream.

In one organization, the dojo discovered that teams wanted to enhance very particular skills. The dojo staff decided to schedule "lab hours" twice a week, and each week they offer a different topic. One week the topic might be deploying to Kubernetes; teams that want to learn about the new deployment strategy would come hang out in the dojo for the scheduled time and ask the dojo coaches specific questions about the topic.

As technology changes, organizations instinctively know they should leverage new technology but don't know how. Artificial intelligence and machine learning (AI/ML) are creating new opportunities for organizations, but the vast majority of engineers aren't skilled in those topics. Your dojo could gain expertise in AI/ML and help teams adopt the new technologies or other new approaches to problem-solving. If coaches in the dojo keep an eye on what's coming next, either they can learn new skills themselves or the organization can bring new people into the dojo who have that knowledge. If you intentionally schedule downtime for coaches, they can use that time to upskill themselves.

The dojo should apply the principles of the dojo to itself. On an ongoing basis, dojo staff should ask themselves:

- What's working?
- What's not working?
- What do we need to adjust?
- What practices do we want to support now?
- What practices do we want to support next?
- What practices do we want to support later?

Don't wait until the teams in your organization lose interest in the dojo; stay ahead of the curve and use the information you gather from teams as they go through the dojo experience to continuously learn about and improve your product.

THE DOJO IS NEVER DONE

A company could send all of its tens of thousands of developers through the dojo. In theory, once all the teams go through the dojo and truly adopt the principles to incorporate learning into their everyday style of working, the dojo's mission would be complete.

The reality is that the need for a dojo never goes away.

Technology changes, practices and methodologies evolve, people retire, and new employees come on board. The need will always be there for a way to upskill people in your organization.

As we've stated previously, we're uncomfortable with the idea of "transformations" as they imply an end state. Learning and experimenting never stop. Don't look for an end, be happy continuously evolving.

We have been working in dojos for five years and are excited to see what the future brings.

TIME TO CHANGE

When teams go through a dojo experience and word of the dojo begins to spread, the dojo becomes a hub where other things start to happen. We've seen organizations have hackathons where teams spend two days working on ideas through rapid experimentation. Other companies organize internal conferences where speakers present ideas, new technologies, and practices. Some dojos decide to schedule a day for sharing code and working on open-source projects together.

All these activities promote the dojo as a space of learning and change—the dojo provides the space, networking, coaching, and facilitation for these things to happen.

Wouldn't you like to see that in your organization?

Your dojo doesn't have to be perfect from day one, but we encourage you to aim high for the long term. In the same way that teams come in to learn and improve, you'll learn and improve on how to run your dojo.

Execution is better than perfection: start with some small experiments with a few teams rather than spending six months trying to put together the perfect dojo. Product delivery demands will continue to increase. Teams have to learn the practices, processes, and technologies to support those demands. Their learning won't happen overnight, nor will the need for learning ever end.

You will learn a lot from the first team. You'll quickly learn the qualities of a good dojo experience and can make adjustments going forward to work with subsequent teams that come into the dojo. There is no perfect time to start the dojo—start now and start learning.

You can do it with this book. We've given you an approach that's worked for multiple dojos. Now go out and learn.

ACKNOWLEDGMENTS

Dion Stewart

I'd like to say thank you to Joel Tosi for going on this adventure with me and being patient with my perfectionist tendencies. I'm looking forward to going on this journey together as we build a community around creating dojos. Rock on!

Thanks to Robert Fripp for teaching me about craft and immersive learning.

Thanks to Dave West for teaching me how to do object-oriented development the right way, for teaching me about the art of software development, and for inspiring many of the ideas I have on how to run dojos.

Michael Nygard—thank you for twenty years of friendship, for teaching me everything I know about software architecture, and for patiently answering every single one of my questions.

I'd also like to thank Istvan Csicsery-Ronay, Etti de Laczay, Jim Beatty, Mark Kassel, and Jason Selby for your friendship and support over the years.

To Jenny Quillien—thanks for the conversations around dojo spaces and coaching.

Finally, thanks to Marc Stock for always keeping me honest. I miss you, my friend.

Joel Tosi

Thanks first and foremost to my partner in crime for this book—Dion Stewart. From the obvious pairing on the ideas in the book to the behind-the-scenes work as my English professor, I can't imagine this book coming to life with anyone other than you, dude. It has been a pleasure. Here's to the future!

To my mother, who taught me perseverance, and my siblings, who have supported me through the years (and didn't tell Mom when I quit my "regular" job to try this independent consulting thing)—thanks for always being there.

To my extended families—the Tintaris, Haskells, and Newhuis—for all of the wonderful family support and good times through the years. I can't wait until we finally buy Spano's and put in the Lord of the Rings go-kart track. For all the readers: mention this book and the vegan doughnuts and BBQ are on me.

Michael Minella—you beat me to the book by a few years—thanks for the inspiration and the good chats.

Dion and Joel

Many of the thoughts in this book we owe to our dear friend, David Hussman, the original "Dude." We're grateful for all the conversations and interesting questions—always challenging us to look deeper and to be more than even we thought we could be. Though you left us in 2018, your impact is still being felt, dude.

To some of the original dojo peeps—Ross Clanton, Stacie Peterson, David Laribee—it has been great sharing and growing these ideas with you through the years. To Jen Guerra, Roger Servey, and Jacki Damiano—thanks for allowing us to continue and evolve the vision.

Thanks to Jeff Patton, Woody Zuill, Kent Beck, Michael Feathers, Mark Graban, Mary and Tom Poppendieck, Bill Allen, and Purple for the encouragement and support.

To our good friend and talented illustrator, Jeremy Kriegel. Thanks for understanding the tone and intention of the book and giving it some great character with your sketches.

To the Dojo Consortium members—thank you for giving us the opportunity to build a community together.

To the wonderful coaches, teams, and people we have met at all the dojos we've worked in—we have learned more from you than you can possibly imagine.

Last, and certainly not least, thanks to our wonderful editor, Barbara Boyd. You were able to not only help us stay focused on the outcomes we were going for with the book, but your probing questions and guidance in simplifying our message made the book something special to us.

Made in the USA
Columbia, SC
16 July 2023